THE
RIGHTS
OF MAN
TODAY

About the Book and Author

The Rights of Man Today
Louis Henkin

Human rights are the idea of our time, but despite the confident words of the U.S. Bill of Rights, the French Declaration on the Rights of Man, and the Universal Declaration, they have not fared well either in principle or in fact. Political, philosophical, and legal controversies have challenged the principle; slavery, ghettos, and mass murders have denied it in fact. Today human rights are everywhere acknowledged as "good"—yet they continue to be a source of confusion and a focus of controversy. This volume explores the contemporary effort to establish and maintain these rights. Professor Henkin analyzes the evolution of the idea of human rights, the "universalization" of human rights as reflected in the spread of "constitutionalism" to almost all of today's 150 states, and the status of human rights in both principle and fact in various nation-states, with emphasis on the U.S. He also examines the "internationalization" of human rights—the movement to promote and protect them by intergovernmental influence—the significance of this effort, and the degree of its success. He closes with a look ahead at the actions that might be taken and the conditions that must exist if the rights of men and women are to be more secure in the future than they are today.

Louis Henkin is Hamilton Fish Professor of International Law and Diplomacy, professor of constitutional law, and also a director of the Center for the Study of Human Rights at Columbia University. His extensive legal experience includes service at the U.N. and in the U.S. Department of State. Professor Henkin is currently president of the U.S. Institute of Human Rights and codirector of the Columbia Center for the Study of Human Rights.

THE
RIGHTS
OF MAN
TODAY

Louis Henkin

Westview Press / Boulder, Colorado

Copyright © 1978 by Westview Press

Published in 1978 in the United States of America by
  Westview Press, Inc.
  5500 Central Avenue
  Boulder, Colorado 80301
  Frederick A. Praeger, Publisher

Library of Congress Cataloging in Publication Data
Henkin, Louis.
  The rights of man today.
  1. Civil rights. I. Title.
JC571.H387   323.4   78-6722
ISBN 0-89158-174-X

Printed and bound in the United States of America

CONTENTS

ACKNOWLEDGMENTS

This volume derives from lectures delivered at Yeshiva University as Benjamin Gottesman Lectures, a series established by Mr. Gottesman's family on the occasion of his seventieth birthday and in recognition of his long interest in the university of which he has been a trustee for more than fifty years.

According to the university's announcement, Gottesman Lectures are intended to be of "scholarly and creative significance" and should "broaden the focus of academic inquiry and explore implications for larger intellectual and social problems." The charge was challenging, and I was grateful for the opportunity.

L. H.

INTRODUCTION

Thomas Paine wrote *The Rights of Man* in 1791-1792, in answer to Edmund Burke's attack on the French Revolution. The principles that Paine defended, as reflected in the first French constitution and the Declaration of the Rights of Man and of the Citizen, owed much to the American Declaration of Independence and to the Virginia Declaration of Rights, now two hundred years old.[1]

The rights of man* were conceived long ago, but they did not duly quicken and mature. At home, in England, Paine was prosecuted for his "wicked seditious writings," was declared an outlaw while out of the country, and never returned. In France, the Revolution ended in the Terror and Napoleonic imperialism. Even in the United States, where the Declaration of Independence was early domesticated in state and national constitutions and bills of rights,[2] the Alien and Sedition Laws came soon after; and the Supreme Court invoked the national Bill of Rights only once before the Civil War, to protect the master's property rights in a famous slave, Dred Scott.[3] Around the world, the United States Bill of Rights and the American and French declarations were widely quoted and copied; Lord

---

*And woman. For me, and I believe for Paine, *man* here corresponds to the German *Mensch*, not to *Mann*. In the words of that legendary English statute, in these pages *man* shall embrace woman.

Acton declared that the single page of print that was the French Declaration "outweighs libraries, and is stronger than all the armies of Napoleon."[4] But these principles did not topple and eliminate all emperors and tsars and dictators; they did not quickly end slavery, torture or cruel punishment, racial or religious discrimination, or political repression and censorship; they did not prevent ghettos or pogroms, or, in our seared memory, the unspeakable, deliberate murders of people and peoples.

The rights of man fared no better in principle than in fact. Thomas Paine's defense of French revolutionary principles is eloquent, and we today might find his reply to Burke devastating, but in his time, and even more recently, not all agreed that Paine won the argument. The rights of man, rooted in axioms of individual autonomy, popular sovereignty, and social contract, were rejected, of course, by those who apotheosized the state and its sovereignty. Their philosophical foundations in natural law and natural rights were scorned even by "progressive" radicals such as Jeremy Bentham, to whom "Natural rights is simple nonsense: natural and imprescriptible rights, rhetorical nonsense—nonsense upon stilts," indeed, mischievous and dangerous nonsense, "anarchical fallacies" encouraging insurrection and resistance to government and to law.[5] For some of the burgeoning socialisms of the nineteenth century, emphasis on the individual and his rights was a diversionary illusion.

Now, much is changed. Today *human rights* is a term in common use in many languages, in the rhetoric of national politics everywhere and of international diplomacy, in the learned jargon of several professions and academic disciplines. All civilizations proclaim their dedication to them; all the major religions proudly lay claim to fathering them; every political leader and would-be leader makes them his platform. What the United States (borrowing from its English mother) and France planted and disseminated now decorates almost every constitution of today's 150 states—old or new, conservative or liberal or radical, capitalist or socialist or mixed, developed or less developed, or underdeveloped. Human rights are now also established in international law, are the subject of numerous treaties and conventions, and are the business of every foreign office and of numerous intergovernmental bodies and nongovernmental organizations. Even philosophers, if not all persuaded, have muted their agnosticism and moved their inquiries to less fundamental planes.[6]

Human rights, we must conclude, have now become for everyone, everywhere, a "good"; by some definitions, indeed, human rights are everything good in human life and society. And yet human rights continue to be a source of confusion and a focus of controversy. Philosophers still dispute, and lawyers still litigate, about them. Many constitutions do not mean what they seem to say, or reflect aspiration but surely not reality. After more than thirty years of determined international effort, human rights are faring poorly in many countries, and leave at least a little to be desired in every country. Every government is accused, by its own citizens and by others, of violating human rights. In the United Nations, alleged violations provide full-time activity for several bodies; and some violations—e.g., in southern Africa—are a principal concern of the major UN organs. In the 1970s human rights became a central issue in U.S. relations with the Soviet Union and a preoccupation of U.S. foreign policy generally. Withal, however, injecting human rights into international politics is commonly considered by diplomats to be unsophisticated and officious and, at least until the Carter administration took office in the United States, hardly a government could fairly say that concern for the rights of everyone everywhere was an integral consideration of its foreign policy and of its international relations. Individuals who have devoted themselves to promoting and protecting human rights have been frequently on the verge of despair.

Considering—in the words of the French Declaration—that "ignorance, neglect, or contempt of the rights of man are the sole causes of public misfortune and of the corruption of governments," I seek here to describe and diagnose the effort to establish and maintain human rights in our times. I survey first the evolution of the idea and its emergence from the battlefield of principle out of the controversies of political philosophers, publicists, and constitutional lawyers during two embattled centuries. I then address the "universalization" of human rights as reflected in the spread of "constitutionalism" everywhere, and consider and compare the condition of human rights, in principle and to some extent in fact, in a few nation-states of different political persuasion and hue, with special attention to the United States. A third chapter examines the "internationalization" of human rights, the movement to promote and protect human rights by intergovernmental influence and international institutions, the significance of this effort, and its successes and disappointments. Finally I venture a hesitant look ahead, identifying the conditions that have to be achieved and the actions that might be taken if the rights of future men and women are to be greater and more secure than our own.

ONE

৸

THE FIRST TWO HUNDRED
YEARS OF AN IDEA

"Rights" have bedeviled legal and political philosophers for centuries,* and the addition of "human" has only caused further uncertainties. There are volumes on the meaning of rights, their source, what gives them authority. There are continuing debates about the relation of rights to duties: Are they exact, verbal correlatives? Can there be a right without a corresponding duty or a duty without a right? Which comes first, the right or the duty (and does it matter)? Can only human beings have rights, or also animals, trees, and corporations, society, the state, the government, even God?** Can one have rights in the abstract or only against somebody; only against another person, or also against the state, the government or its officials, against oneself, or even against God? Does a person alone on an island have rights and, if so, against whom?

Most of these jurisprudential inquiries are not material to the law, the politics, or the sociology of human rights in our day. For our purposes, human rights are claims asserted and

---

*Confusion has been aggravated by linguistic development, itself perhaps significant. Some languages give *rights* several different though not unrelated meanings—legal, moral, logical, or conventional. In English we have, variously and among others: "I have a right to that book"; "he was right to disobey the law"; "that is a right answer."

**Justice Douglas has suggested that environmental issues might be litigated in the name of "the inanimate object about to be . . . despoiled," with those who have an "intimate relation" with it recognized as its legitimate spokesmen.[1]

1

recognized "as of right," not claims upon love, or grace, or brotherhood, or charity: one does not have to earn or deserve them. They are not merely aspirations or moral assertions but, increasingly, legal claims under some applicable law.

Human rights, I stress, are rights against society as represented by government and its officials. One may conclude that government must protect the individual from neighbors or from wolves, that it must afford legal remedies against a wrongdoer, that it must provide bread or free hospitalization; but, at bottom, the rights claimed are against the state, not against the neighbor or the wolves, the wrongdoer, the baker, or the hospital. In the eighteenth century human rights were thought of as limitations on what government might do to the individual; today they also include what society is deemed obligated to do for the individual. Here human rights are not in contradistinction to human liberties: they include the right to be free, and not only "free from," but also "free to"; they include not only rights to do, but also rights to have and to be.

I write of claims against society; perhaps one should speak rather of claims upon society. For human rights are not perceived as "against society," against the interest of society; in the theology of human rights, the good society is one in which individual rights flourish, and the promotion and protection of individual rights are a public good. There is an aura of conflict between individual and society only in that individual rights are asserted against government, against those who represent society officially, and it is sometimes necessary to choose between an individual's right and some other public good. By the ideology of rights, in this choice individual rights cannot be lightly sacrificed even for the greater good of the greater number, even for the general good of all. Government cannot do some things, and must do others, even though officials are persuaded that it is in the society's interest (and even in the individual's own interest) to do otherwise. But this conflict between individual and society is only temporary and superficial; in the longer, deeper view, the society is better if the individual's right is respected.

That the rights we are describing are "human" has additional intrinsic implications. They are the rights of men and women. These may assert the right to worship God, form associations, own or protect animals or trees; but neither God, the association, the animal, or the tree has human rights. The concept has also acquired connotations and overtones. These are rights that all human beings everywhere have—or should have—equally and in equal measure by virtue of their humanity; regardless of sex, race, perhaps also of age; regardless of high or low "birth," social class, national origin, ethnic or tribal affiliation; regardless of wealth or poverty, occupation, talent, merit, religion, ideology, or other commitment. (A person may have additional legal rights by virtue of some of these extraneous qualities, or of others such as citizenship, residence, or having been elected to office. But those are not "human rights.") If these rights are implied in one's humanity, they are inalienable. They cannot be transferred, forfeited, or waived; they are "imprescriptible," that is, they cannot be lost by having been usurped or by failure to exercise or assert them, no matter for how long.

It is also commonly said that human rights are "fundamental." That may imply only that they are important, that life, dignity, and other high human values depend on them. It does not mean that they are absolute and may never be abridged for any purpose in any circumstances; it means that they are entitled to special protection enjoying at least a prima facie, presumptive inviolability, bowing only to compelling societal interests, in limited circumstances, for limited times and purposes, and by limited means.

Origins and Antecedents

The conception of human rights as an individual's political-legal claims, implying limitations and obligations upon society and government, is a product of modern history. It reflects particular political theories and rejects others. Both the recent history and the prevailing theory reflect their ante-cedents.

The origins and ancestry of ideas are rarely single or simple, or readily disentangled. Many can claim patent to the ideas of human rights, with some warrant, yet all claims include some exaggeration, for the various elements of human rights have different ancestry, and attempts to correlate contemporary with ancient concepts court anachronism and other distortion. The Bible, for example, stressed not rights but duties—and these were essentially duties to God, although fellow man was the beneficiary of many of them.[2] "Society" and "government" were not central conceptions in the life of a people governed by God through his prophets, judges, and others chosen, ordained, or anointed. (The people's desire for a king was decried as a rejection of God's kingship.)[3] The "higher law," God's law, was in principle the only law. The individual had free will and freedom of choice; but he was, a priori, not autonomous but subject to God's law, and he was not to do "that which was right in his own eyes."[4] On the other hand, the major religions, philosophies, and poetic traditions can surely claim some ideas and values central to human rights: right and wrong, good and evil; law, legality, and illegality, justice and fairness; the equal protection of the laws; the significance of individual man and the essential dignity and equality of men. In the Bible, justice is particularized in various precepts but is also prescribed generally, undefined but intuitive, and is required of God as of man.[5] The equality and dignity of man are supported by the Genesis story of the common ancestor of mankind and by the fatherhood of God to all men.[6] For the principle of limited, "constitutional" government—that there is a higher law binding on the governor as on the governed, and that man-made law is valid and to be respected only insofar as it is consistent with that higher law—we cite Sophocles's Antigone, the midwives resisting Pharaoh's order to kill all male Israelite babies, King Saul's servants refusing to kill the priests, or the story of Daniel.[7]

Immediately, human rights derive from "natural rights" flowing from "natural law."[8] The Stoics, Cicero, and their jurist successors did not perceive natural law as a higher law invalidating and justifying disobedience to man-made laws that did not measure up, but as a standard for making, developing, and interpreting law: law should be made and developed so that it will correspond to nature.[9] Later the church christianized Roman ideas, rooted natural law in divine authority, and gave it the quality of highest law. Although some of this law was revealed, most of it was left to man to uncover and develop by his God-given "right reason."

Natural law theory emphasized duties imposed by God on every human society in an orderly cosmos. In time, society's duties came to be seen as natural rights for the individual. It was difficult, however, to fill early natural rights with agreed content, other, perhaps, than the rights of "conscience"—to worship the true God and to refuse to commit "unjust" acts.

Currents of natural law and natural rights run deep in human rights even today.[10] Politically as well as intellectually, however, human rights today trace their authentic origins to seventeenth- and eighteenth-century concepts. Although no idea is nicely confined within dates, although each recent century saw variety in ideas, one might see human rights today as a kind of twentieth-century synthesis of an eighteenth-century thesis and a nineteenth-century antithesis.

The Eighteenth-Century Thesis

The American and French revolutions, and the declarations that expressed the principles that inspired them, took "natural rights" and made them secular, rational, universal, individual, democratic, and radical. For divine foundations for the rights of man they substituted (or perhaps only added) a social-contractual base. Consider these famous lines:

We hold these truths to be self-evident, that all men are created equal, that they are endowed by their creator with certain unalienable rights, that among these are life, liberty and the pursuit of happiness. That to secure these rights, governments are instituted among men, deriving their just powers from the consent of the governed, that . . . it is the right of the people . . . to institute new government, laying its foundation on such principles, and organizing its power in such form, as to them shall seem most likely to effect their safety and happiness.[11]

The Virginia Declaration of Rights begins:

1. That all men are by nature equally free and independent, and have certain inherent rights, of which, when they enter into a state of society, they cannot, by any compact, deprive or divest their posterity; namely, the enjoyment of life and liberty, with the means of acquiring and possessing property, and pursuing and obtaining happiness and safety.

2. That all power is vested in, and consequently derived from, the people; that magistrates are their trustees and servants, and at all times amenable to them.

3. That government is, or ought to be, instituted for the common benefit, protection, and security of the people, nation, or community; of all the various modes and forms of government, that is best which is capable of producing the greatest degree of happiness and safety, and is most effectually secured against the danger of maladministration; and that, when any government shall be found inadequate or contrary to these purposes, a majority of the community hath an undubitable inalienable, and indefeasible right to reform, alter, or abolish it, in such manner as shall be judged most conducive to the public weal.

The rights of man, it will be noted, are not (or not necessarily) divinely ordained, not (or not necessarily) divinely conceived: they are God's gift in that they result from his creation.* They are natural in the sense that nature (and

---

*The relation of these rights to God is ambiguous. In the American declaration, men are endowed with rights by their creator. That may mean what Paine meant when he referred to the "illuminating and divine principle of equal rights of man, (for it has its origin from the Maker of man)"; therefore, "all men are born equal, and with equal natural right."[12] The French Declaration was made only "in the presence and under the auspices of the Supreme Being."

nature's God) created and inspired man's reason and judgment. They are natural in the sense that every man is born with them. They are natural also in a different sense, in that they are man's in the "state of nature," and he brings them with him into society. The individual was autonomous, sovereign, before government was established, and he, and other individuals taken together—"the people"—remain sovereign under any government, for their sovereignty is inalienable, and government is only by the consent of the governed. (The logical leap from autonomy of the individual to the sovereignty of the people and majority rule was not commonly noted or explained; presumably that was deemed implicit in the social compact.)

The people gave up some of their autonomy to government for limited purposes, retaining the rest as rights and freedoms under government. (Paine distinguished "that class of natural rights which man retains after entering society, and those which he throws into common stock as a member of society" because he cannot execute them by himself.[13] Rights originate with and are retained by the people; they are not granted to them.* "Society *grants* him nothing. Every man is a proprietor in society, and draws on the capital as a matter of right."[15] Some rights, indeed, could not be subordinated to government even if the people wished, because these rights are inalienable.

Man retains rights against government in principle by virtue of his social contract, though that, we know, is a hypothetical construct, not a historical fact; a justification, not an explanation.[16] In any particular society, the rights retained

---

*Compare the Ninth Amendment to the United States Constitution: "The enumeration in the Constitution, of certain rights, shall not be construed to deny or disparage others retained by the people." Explicit provisions of the Bill of Rights also reflect the view that rights are not bestowed by the Constitution but are antecedent to it; the Bill of Rights only commands the government to respect those antecedent rights. E.g., "Congress shall make no law . . . abridging the freedom of speech, or of the press." "The right of the people to be secure . . . shall not be violated." Amendments I, IV. The Supreme Court has written of "implied reservations of individual rights, without which the social compact could not exist."[14]

may be determined by "the people" in an actual contract with their government. In the United States, for example, we look for our rights in the people's contract with their governors, in the Constitution, which "We the people . . . ordain and establish."[17]

Inevitably the rights retained are the preferred, contemporary values, though the founding fathers, and the people they represent, may deem and justify them as "natural," the inspiration of nature and of nature's God. Although in principle the people must retain those rights that are "inalienable," which rights are inalienable will be determined by what the people (or those who draft their constitutions) in fact decide to retain. Whatever the source from which rights draw their inspiration, then, in this view the authority for rights, and their content, are contractual.

The people, of course, may deem and justify their values as eternal and their rights as timeless, valid for their children's children as for themselves. But in principle, surely, the autonomy and sovereignty of our ancestors did not include the right to impose their values on their descendants.* Later generations might decide that their ancestors improperly alienated the inalienable, or that they might delegate to their government new kinds of authority and new responsibilities and retain less autonomy for themselves. It was perhaps permissible for our ancestors to make the United States Constitution valid indefinitely, and even difficult to amend. But we are as autonomous as our ancestors, our reason is as right as theirs, and their own principles would warrant us in tearing up the Constitution and substituting our own terms with government, terms that would reflect our views of its proper purposes and retain the rights and liberties that we would not alienate.

---

*Thomas Paine rejected Burke's notion that the people were bound by agreements made by their ancestors, whether with king or with parliament: "The vanity and presumption of governing beyond the grave, is the most ridiculous and insolent of all tyrannies."[18]

The American fathers of rights were not legal philosophers. They were not troubled to debate against whom an individual has these rights, what duties they imply, and upon whom they fell. They did not ask whether they were only moral rights or also legal rights, and if the latter, under what system of law. They did not consider it relevant to indicate how such legal rights could be enforced. Presumably they saw these rights as implying duties of restraint upon their chosen governors, and some restraints might be mandated by the courts of law. We know they saw their rights as justifying "self-determination," independence from Great Britain. In principle "the people"— though not particular individuals—could vindicate their rights by revolution and reconstitution.

The Content of Eighteenth-Century Rights

The eighteenth-century birth date of human rights, of course, shaped their content. They were the rights that the wise men thought the people wished to retain, or thought they should retain and persuaded them to do so, the rights that reflected their views of the purposes of government and the desirable division of authority between government and individual. For these views, those who drafted the various declarations and constitutions and those—like Thomas Paine—who preached and propagated their principles drew principally on John Locke (perhaps filtered through Blackstone), Montesquieu, and Rousseau,* with perspective, detail, and emphasis from their own experience.

Locke gave us essential ideas out of English antecedents,** including probably those of the Levellers.[21] Some go back to the hallowed Great Charter, to Magna Carta, to what it was,

---

*To Rousseau one might trace the view that men were created equal, that they were autonomous before they entered into society, and that their submission to society is governed by the social contract.[19]

**Although the eighteenth century drew immediately on the seventeenth, more or less authentic antecedents for the several doctrines reflected in the Declaration of Independence have been traced back to old sources. One author found the creation of

perhaps more to what it was perceived, even misperceived, to
be. Perhaps all that happened in 1215 at Runnymede was that
some nobles stood up to King John, broke his autarchy, and
exacted some concessions for themselves. Even that, obviously,
was a limitation on monarchy and a seed of constitutionalism.
Rights that the nobles obtained for themselves, later, slowly,
spread to others: unknowing, the nobles laid the foundations
for parliament. A perhaps innocent, incidental phrase in
Magna Carta, providing that a freeman shall be punished only
"by the lawful judgment of his peers or by the law of the land,"
came to establish the rule of law; later that became the "due
process of law," with its luxuriant growth in U.S. constitutional jurisprudence.[22] From subsequent components of the
British constitution—the Petition of Rights (1628), the
Agreement of the People (1647), the Bill of Rights (1688)—the
eighteenth century developed representative government,
expanded suffrage and increased protections for those whom
authority accused of crime, and established some freedom of
religion and some freedom from religious discrimination.

The rights of man were born in revolution, against Great
Britain here, against the *ancien régime* in France. Inevitably
they were political rights, and self-government and the consent
to be governed were their essential character. To Thomas
Paine, representative government was *the* human right:
"representative government is freedom."[23] But the framers of
rights were not content with democracy, even with representative government, for parliament, too, they had learned, could
be despotic: "The accumulation of all powers, legislative,
executive, and judiciary, in the same hands, whether of one, a
few, or many, and whether hereditary, self-appointed, or
elective, may justly be pronounced the very definition of

----

government as a conscious act, and the social compact, in Protagoras and the Sophists
(as reflected in Plato's *Republic*); government as based on the consent of the governed,
and the right of revolution, in St. Augustine; natural, inalienable rights in Cicero and
the Roman jurists Gaius and Ulpian; equality in the Stoics and in Wycliffe; and the
combination of the various doctrines, as in the Declaration of Independence, in
Nicholas of Cusa.[20]

tyranny."[24] Hence the separation of powers and checks and balances that have remained our particular U.S. hallmark— not, Justice Brandeis reminded us, to promote efficiency, but to prevent tyranny.[25] Our federalism, too, was a "vertical separation," which by dividing authority guarded against too much, too concentrated governmental power.[26] And against any and all government the individual retains his other inviolable rights.*

Locke wrote of the rights of life, liberty, and property; the Declaration of Independence spoke of life, liberty, and the pursuit of happiness. (Locke sometimes spoke of property as including individual autonomy and it is not implausible to argue that even when used more narrowly, *property* did not reflect narrow concern for the property of "men of property," but regarded rights to personal possessions and the fruits of one's labor as aspects of individuality and autonomy—and the pursuit of happiness?—for all.) The United States Constitution guaranteed neither of these formulas of rights, for the Constitution, as conceived, was not essentially a charter of rights and liberties, but a blueprint of government.** The Constitution, moreover, largely governed only the new federal government, which at our beginnings was not the principal government on these shores, but only a small superstructure on the governments of the states. It was the states that governed

---

*Compare Mr. Justice Miller: "A government which recognized no such rights, which held the lives, the liberty, and the property of its citizens subject at all times to the absolute disposition and unlimited control of even the most democratic depository of power, is after all but a despotism. It is true it is a despotism of the many, of the majority, if you choose to call it so, but it is none the less a despotism. It may well be doubted if a man is to hold all that he is accustomed to call his own, all in which he has placed his happiness, and the security of which is essential to that happiness, under the unlimited dominion of others, whether it is not wiser that this power should be exercised by one man than by many."[27]

**We tend to couple the Declaration and the Constitution in our national hagiography, but they are, of course, different in inspiration, purpose, tone, and character. The Declaration was a ringing manifesto heralding and justifying revolution; the Constitution was a blueprint of government. Perhaps all postrevolutionary constitutions are inherently "conservative," seeking to conserve and to establish what antecedent revolutions fought for, although ours has impressed many as strikingly

individual lives intimately, every day, and it is primarily to the states' constitutions and bills and declarations of rights that one must go to see what rights the people had. These, and those included later in the national Bill of Rights, contained the political rights we know—political freedom, security and privacy, rights for those accused of crime. They reflected an ideology of rights that implied original individual autonomy subject only to limited government for limited purposes.* Government, and every act of government, had to be justified. The individual was protected against his government; there was no suggestion that he could make claim on government to contribute to his economic and social welfare. The Constitution was ordained, inter alia, "to promote the general welfare," and Congress could lay and collect taxes to provide for "the general welfare."[29] But neither the framers of the federal constitution nor those who established the governments of the states considered it to be a purpose of government to provide the citizen with food or work or social security. (Only the obligation to provide or promote education found its way early into some state constitutions.)[30]

Note a glaring (and unhappy) omission. The original U.S. Constitution did not ordain equality. Some of the early state constitutions did declare the equality of all men, but such declarations had no normative significance. States that declared equality maintained slavery. (The Indians also enjoyed

---

removed from the spirit of 1776, responding to years of frustration with the difficulties of self-governance and hammered out in careful compromise. Originally, the Constitution did not even have a bill of rights because the framers thought it unnecessary, since the limited powers of the federal government would hardly impinge on the individual and his rights.[28] The bill of rights was added by amendment under the new government, as promised, the price of ratification in several states.

*Compare Jefferson's First Inaugural Address: "Still one thing more, fellow citizens—a wise and frugal Government, which shall restrain men from injuring one another, shall leave them otherwise free to regulate their own pursuits of industry and improvement, and shall not take from the mouth of labor the bread it has earned. This is the sum of good government, and this is necessary to close the circle of our felicities."

less than equality, although their situation was more ambiguous since in many respects they were autonomous and not part of U.S. society.) There was not full equality even among freemen, between propertied and propertyless, between men and women, even in the measure we know today.

Note, on the other hand, what today might seem a striking but happy omission. A constitution ordained by the people to prescribe and limit their government does not provide for its suspension, or for government by decree even in emergency. It does not declare the people's duties or make their rights contingent on the performance of duties.[31]

The French Legacy

Americans tend to think of human rights as their special gift to the world. Even if we include our English ancestors and cousins in that self-congratulation, it is egoistically blind at least by half. The eighteenth-century ideology of rights drew on French as well as English ideas, and the French Revolution and Declaration were probably more influential than ours in spreading them in many parts of the world. The French Declaration, moreover, articulated some ideas that were at best implicit with us, such as the presumption of innocence.[32] It propagated also ideas more "advanced" than our own, some of which took long to reach and take root in the United States. "Liberty consists in the power to do anything that does not injure another." "The law has the right to forbid only such actions as are injurious to society." "All citizens . . . are equally eligible to all public dignities, places and employments, according to their capacities and without other distinction than their virtues and their talents." Taxes should be "equally apportioned among all the citizens according to their means."[33] And the French constitution of 1791 provided for public relief for the poor and free public education— "economic and social rights" unknown in early U.S. constitutions.

A Nineteenth-Century Antithesis

The nineteenth century also contributed importantly to human rights. To the conception of natural rights, rationalized by the eighteenth century in social contract, the nineteenth century added ethical and utilitarian support: rights and freedoms are necessary for the good life in a good society. To some, Darwin may have suggested the survival of the human species as the inspiration of human rights and as a touchstone—perhaps the touchstone—for determining the content of human rights.[34] To the earlier authors of rights—God, the people—the nineteenth century added man and the human psyche: rights and liberties are dictated by the nature of man, by his needs for dignity and fulfillment. The nineteenth century achieved a "breakthrough" in human freedom in the abolition of slavery in many countries and the international prohibition of the slave trade. It gave us the apostle of liberty, John Stuart Mill. In the United States, at least, it also raised high a new freedom—economic liberty and freedom from governmental intervention—generally as preached in England by Herbert Spencer on Adam Smith's texts.[35]

In the large, however, the nineteenth century and the early decades of the twentieth century witnessed continued, even renewed, resistance to human rights. The nineteenth century began with Napoleon, and the Congress of Vienna and later great power concerts were dedicated to "legitimacy," not to the sovereignty of the people and individual rights. The nineteenth century saw the rise of nationalism and the heyday of imperialism. Representative government mushroomed in new soil, as in Latin America, but it did not everywhere strike root and flourish. The first half of the twentieth century saw old autocracies give way to new ones, as in Russia, and substantial democracy give way to the worst of tyrannies, as in Germany, Italy, and Spain.

Where representative government did not prevail, other rights of man surely did not flourish. Even where rights had been established and were healthy, as in the United States, there were weaknesses: slavery ended only after bitter civil war, racial equality was effectively frustrated, political and civil rights for many lay quiescent, and economic liberty also served to support child labor and sweatshops, the right of the laborer to be exploited and the consumer to be milked.[36]

In the realm of ideas, the nineteenth century was as long, as prolific, and as variegated as perhaps any we have known—a century that began in the life of Kant and ran to the death of Nietzsche, that produced Marx and Darwin and Freud, that gave us a score of other "greats" and at least that many philosophical "isms." No single set of ideas dominated the nineteenth century; surely, the century of Bentham and John Stuart Mill, or of the philosophical anarchists, was not ideologically hostile to human freedoms and welfare. But among the many currents of ideas that churned were several that provide an antithesis to the eighteenth-century ideology of individual rights and popular sovereignty: namely, scorn for natural law and natural rights; devotion to activist, not minimalist, government; subordination of the individual to the group, of political and economic liberty—especially laissez-faire—to the pursuit of common good of all, or to the greatest good of the greatest number.

The Depreciation of Natural Law

Natural rights were anathema to those to whom the state was all. They were also rejected by highly moral, humane progressives and libertarians as anarchical nonsense. Natural law and natural rights, they might have reminded us, were as often "the shield of arch-conservatism as the sword of radicalism";[37] invoked to justify the divine rights of kings and royal legitimacy, slavery and religious intolerance, manifest destiny and laissez-faire, the natural inferiority of women and of the poor. To Paine, the "Declaration of Rights is of more value to the world, and will do more good, than all the laws and statutes that have yet been promulgated."[38] More nonsense,

Bentham might have said: "What is everyman's right is no man's right."[39] And natural law and rights permit hiding behind empty platitudes to frustrate progress by government and legislation to promote individual welfare and freedom.[40]

Rationalism, secularism, and humanism in the nineteenth century rejected natural rights based on divine natural law; the foundation of rights in the equality of all men as children of God, descended from the common ancestor, was dealt a stunning blow by the theory of evolution. In jurisprudence, natural law suffered the onslaughts of positivism; and who shall arbitrate* between good law and bad law, moral law and immoral law? Law is and can only be the edict of the sovereign;[41] how, then, can there be legal rights against the sovereign?

Socialism and Individualism

A second element of antithesis to eighteenth-century individual rights came from the burgeoning socialisms. Again, I do not suggest that socialism is hostile to human rights; there have been, and are, socialists who are leading proponents of liberty, e.g., John Stuart Mill, and various twentieth-century figures in Great Britain and in Western Europe. Socialism, moreover, is not ideologically pure or single, and different theorists of socialism—and the same theorists at different times—have held widely different views about the rights of the individual in a socialist society, or in bourgeois societies on the way to socialism. But there are strands common to various brands of socialism, and stressed by some socialists, that are antithetical to eighteenth-century emphasis on the rights of the individual. Even for presocialist utilitarianism, presumably, the individual had no claims against "the greatest good of the greatest number." "Socialism," as its etymology suggests,

---

*"Now, who shall arbitrate?/ Ten men love what I hate,/ Shun what I follow, slight what I receive;/ Ten, who in ears and eyes/ Match me: we all surmise,/ They this thing, and I that: whom shall my soul believe?" R. Browning, *Rabbi Ben Ezra.*

emphasizes the society, the group, subordinating the individual or seeing his salvation eventually in the salvation of the group. Christian socialism, while rejecting Marxist materialism, also attacked the individualism and egotism that led to the inequities of capitalist society. For some main branches of Marxism, surely, individual rights in a capitalist society were palliatives, indeed, illusions perpetuating the real evil. The liberation of the individual can come only after the mass has been liberated. "Everything for the mass": true individual welfare could come only after society was cleansed and reordered; then "the narrow bourgeois horizon of rights" can be left far behind and—in a nod to anarchism—the state would wither away and the individual would be free.[42] During progress toward perfect socialism, the socialist state would reject "individualism" and presumably "individual rights." That an individual might have rights against the socialist state was unthinkable. The socialist state knows no a priori limitations of individual autonomy or right on what it may do to realize socialism. Socialism emphasizes not rights against society, but duties to society. The greatest honor is to serve the socialist state. Later, in the twentieth century, the Marxist-Leninist states for many years did not enthrone "the people"; they preferred "the masses." They declared the "dictatorship of the proletariat," which, of course, implied no rights for the nonproletariat, and even for the proletariat only group rights, and only those consistent with socialist purposes.[43]

This socialist antithesis to individual rights implied more than a subordination of individual to group, of rights to duties. It put economic advance before political-civil rights,[44] welfare before and above liberty. It saw the purpose of government not merely, or even primarily, as a "watchdog," to maximize security, liberty, autonomy, governing best when it governed least; instead, government was to act, to intervene, to plan, to promote, to direct, to do. If such socialism resorted at all to the language of rights, it asserted them not as limitations on

government but as obligations upon it, not freedom from
government but demands upon it. It evoked not a right to think
or speak or assemble, or even to be secure, but a right to work
and eat.

The Twentieth-Century Synthesis

The twentieth century brought new and changing political
contexts for human rights and transformed the philosophical
and ideological debates about them. The decades bridging the
nineteenth and twentieth centuries saw new assaults upon
human rights as well as new attempts to establish them. A
demand for "constitutionalism" was heard in the Russian and
Austrian empires, but it was soon overwhelmed by world wars
and the emergence of totalitarian socialist and "national-
socialist" states. Allied victory in World War II ended Hitler's
terrible atrocities and launched a vast international human
rights campaign and program. The emergence of the Soviet
Union and the People's Republic of China as world powers led
to ideological conflict between them and Western democracy;
conceptions of human rights were a principal issue, but in time
the communists, too, saw fit to claim the mantle of human
rights. The ineluctable drive against colonialism brought a
mass of new states and governments that looked to the idea of
human rights to achieve "self-determination" and the elimination of racism. The Third World also moved to establish
"economic self-determination" and "the New International
Economic Order" and place them high in the human rights
ideology, with important implications in principle and
practice for other, older rights.[45]

Political changes within and between nations in our century
mooted many of the intellectual-ideological differences between the eighteenth and nineteenth centuries. Nineteenth-
century "legitimacy," the all-powerful state, extremes of
nationalism and sovereignty, are no longer in fashion. The
sovereignty of the people is denied nowhere, asserted every-

where, even in some states that began as dictatorships of the proletariat. Suffrage is everywhere universal and government is representative, although the forms that suffrage and representation take in many countries might have seemed as fraudulent to Thomas Paine as they do to many Western observers today. Everywhere there are constitutions, and all constitutions proclaim liberties, equality, justice, although these may mean different things in different places, and although countries also differ widely in the measure in which these constitutional promises are realized.[46]

From Natural to Positive Law

Perhaps the most striking philosophical development in recent decades is the quiescence of positivism and the reanimation of natural law and natural rights.[47] Positivists, often highly moral and humane, could not comfortably proclaim the equal validity of all law in the face of Hitler's "lawful" abominations, and philosophers of democracy have asserted the "natural" legitimacy of positive law only when made by representative democratic majorities. In our own day "civil disobedience," especially in relation to the Vietnam war, gave renewed discredit to positivism, gave renewed respectability to a "natural law" higher even than the law of democratic majorities.

It is not moral and political embarrassment alone that has muted the philosophical distaste and discredit for natural rights. Political forces have mooted the principal philosophical objections, bridging the chasm between natural and positive law by converting natural human rights into positive legal rights.*

The way was shown in the very infancy of constitutionalism by our own constitutional fathers and by John Marshall, chief

---

*In every legal system, of course, many "natural rights" are incorporated into, or given effect by, legislation or (as in the British tradition) by common law. But these have no status as higher law and could be withdrawn by subsequent law. I write here of rights given status as higher law.

justice of the United States. The framers declared the
Constitution to be the "law of the land," like laws made by the
legislature.[48] But the Constitution is a higher law, not higher
law left to divination from revelation or to development by
right reason, but a higher positive law ordained by the ultimate
legislature, the sovereign people. And, John Marshall established, the Constitution, and the limitations on government
implied in the blueprint of government and expressed in the
Bill of Rights, are to be applied and enforced by the courts
against the political branches of the government of the United
States (and of the states).[49] In time, the emergence of a trusted
institution to monitor the limitations on government encouraged abandoning precise lines and sharp distinctions
between the domains of individual and government and
substituting a "balancing" of private rights and public good.

A positive higher law, binding and enforceable against the
government! Americans now take it for granted, and others
have found it appealing, but it is a startling notion and is far
from being universally accepted or appreciated. It was
politically and philosophically daring of Marshall, although it
was perhaps made easier for him: we were a new, and a new
kind of, nation, the first conceived in constitutionalism; and
the implications of that conception were inchoate, yet to be
developed by bold and prescient spirits. It was easier for
Marshall, too, to enforce the Constitution as higher positive
law because the notion of a higher law—a higher natural law—
was not foreign to him. (He might have been prepared to refuse
effect to laws as contrary to natural law if the Constitution had
not been available to serve similar purpose.)[50] Nineteenth-
century positivists might challenge the very title of "constitutional law," insisting that it is not, and cannot be, law because
it is not the edict of the effective sovereign. They might dismiss
the sovereignty of "the people," and the suggestion that the
sovereign people enacted the Constitution, as mere rhetoric.
They might add that law binding on the government is a
contradiction and nonsense. But in the United States, surely,

constitutional law is law by almost any definition; powerful presidents, commanding huge armies, have bowed to the decree of the Supreme Court with its single, unarmed marshal.[51]

That judicial review, with the courts conclusively declaring the limits of government, would become the established way of the United States was not obvious or inevitable. It was challenged by presidents and by congresses and by states, as well as by students of the Constitution, in Marshall's time and still in our century, as recently as the days of the New Deal and racial desegregation.[52] But Marshall has prevailed, and judicial review has spread, if with indigenous variations, to every continent—to Latin America, Europe, Australia, even to new states in Asia and Africa—and in a substantial number of countries, human rights are now constitutional rights, positive higher law enforced by the courts.* Many states that were not prepared to make human rights a higher law were impelled to enact them into ordinary law or, at least, accept them as policy and aspiration, imposing effective limits on government, affording effective protection for individual men and women.

The conversion of individual rights from natural to positive law did not eliminate all reliance on natural, "self-evident" principles. The decision to adopt a constitution and give it status as higher law may itself be deemed required by natural law, and the rights enshrined in the constitution may be those believed to be natural rights. Constitutions ordained during the reign of natural law, in particular, may be deemed to have incorporated some of its principles, and Delphic constitutional clauses will be interpreted in their light. So, in the U.S. Constitution, "unreasonable" search and seizure, and "cruel and unusual" punishment or even "due" process of law. Some saw "natural law" when the Supreme Court held that the due process clause forbade that which "shocked the conscience" of

---

*Rights may be enforced by other institutions, e.g., by an ombudsman or procurator general. But these usually protect the individual only against official and bureaucratic abuse. They do not presume to invalidate the acts of legislatures or even of chief executives.

mankind.[53] There are undertones of natural law and natural right in the new right of privacy, a zone of individual autonomy that is "fundamental" and cannot be invaded except for a compelling state interest.[54]

Positive International Law

The transformation of natural rights into positive legal rights took an additional and different step with the development of an international law of human rights.[55] Lawyers and historians debate the authentic origins of this law, and there is also disagreement about its political significance. But there can be no doubt that, surely since World War II, there has been a significant growth of international agreements containing human rights norms binding on the parties; probably, too, there has been a growth of some customary international human rights norms binding on all states. For the international system, the international law of human rights is higher positive law, binding on states that adhere to it regardless of their own constitutions or other laws, and requiring them to conform their laws and their official behavior to the international norm.[56] Nineteenth-century positivists might not be more hospitable to international law than to constitutional law, but again, if the test is whether international law governs state behavior, whether it is largely observed, it is surely effective law.[57]

An international law of human rights strives for universality regardless of historical and cultural differences. Again, for some lawmakers, in some states, the impulse to develop an international positive law of human rights may reflect a sense that such rights are "natural" and required by natural law,[58] and the rights legislated into international law may be those considered natural rights. If most governments and officials who helped make this law responded rather to political forces, whether international or domestic, these forces themselves may be inspired by beliefs that such rights are natural rights.

It is noteworthy that essentially the same political and civil rights and freedoms that the eighteenth century derived from natural right, individual autonomy, and social contract appear in positive law of diverse national systems and of international law. One can debate whether this lends support to the "natural" character of these rights, to their foundation in characteristics common to political societies or in the nature of man; or whether it reflects merely the contemporary appeal of these ideas, the effectiveness of transnational communication, the influence of ideological competition. Whatever its impulses and motivations, the positive international law of human rights, like the positive national law of human rights, did not eliminate all reliance on, or preclude all reference to, nonpositive "natural" principles. The UN Charter is punctuated with references to "justice," to the "fundamental," to "larger freedom." The UN human rights conventions forbid "cruel, inhuman and degrading" treatment; cite the family as a "natural and fundamental" group; require "just and favorable remuneration" for work; and refer to the "just requirements of morality."[59]

When human rights became a subject of international law, it thereby became subject to the international law-making process, a political process in which other interests intruded. To the synthesis of political-civil with economic-social rights, the international process added rights not in any of the national bills of rights, for example, the right to self-determination and to economic self-determination, i.e., national control over a state's natural resources and exclusion of foreign interests. Opponents argued that neither of these was a human right because it was not an individual right but at best the right of a "people" or a "state," but proponents who sought every opportunity to further these causes placed them at the head of both principal UN human rights covenants.

The Second Synthesis: Liberty and Welfare

In addition to both escaping and bridging the dichotomy of natural and positive law, the twentieth century has brought also a marriage, more or less convenient and comfortable, between the emphasis on the individual, his autonomy and liberty, and the emphasis by socialism on the group and on economic and social welfare for all; between the view of government as a threat to liberty, a necessary evil to be resisted and limited, and the view that sees government as a beneficial agency to act vigorously to promote the common welfare.

The fusion did not come easily. Countries with traditions of political liberty and of limited government were hospitable also to notions of economic liberty, laissez-faire, and "social statics," and were hostile to activist, intervening, planning government. Philosophers were troubled: a state can respect liberties; how can it "guarantee" everyone work or food? Is a holiday with pay a universal moral right?[60] But philosophers are not kings, and governors are not philosophers. Today even the United States, Great Britain, France, and other countries of Western Europe are essentially welfare states. These developments, no doubt, owed much to "foreign ideas," to the influence of socialist thought, but they have been given a liberal cast and context. That "a necessitous man is not a free man" was broadcast to the world not by Marx or Lenin but by Franklin Delano Roosevelt, and in the principles he enunciated, principles for which hundreds of millions fought in World War II, "Freedom from Want" ranked equally with "Freedom of Expression and Worship" and "Freedom from Fear." "Full employment" measures that would have imbedded "the right to work" in American ideology were introduced in Congress in 1945, unsuccessfully, but they were again proposed in the late 1970s and are now clearly no longer unthinkable.[61] In the West, at least as much as elsewhere, there is also a growing tendency to see human rights even larger, at least in aspiration, to include all that goes to make up a life of essential human dignity, including autonomy, privacy, idiosyncrasy, self-development, security, peace, a healthy environment, and participation in decisions that affect the individual.

One aspect of this synthesis was the rise of equality as a cardinal human right. Eighteenth-century rights theory had limited conceptions of equality and gave preference to liberty, but nineteenth-century socialism exalted equality and set it high above liberty.* The twentieth century adopted equality and liberty as basic rights and expanded and deepened the eighteenth-century connotations of equality. In the rhetoric of the eighteenth century, equality meant primarily political equality (and not necessarily universal suffrage). The famous assertion in the Declaration of Independence that all men are created equal probably implied also that all men should have equal legal status and equal opportunity. These were brought into law later by the abolition of slavery and by the constitutional mandate of the "equal protection of the laws": government may not discriminate invidiously in any respect on irrelevant grounds, and, in particular, differences of race, religion, or ethnic or national origin are generally irrelevant.[63] The twentieth century has deepened that "equal protection" by holding government responsible for some unofficial discriminations; by rejecting "ingenious as well as ingenuous" forms of separation and distinction; by reexamining stereotypical and other accepted bases for distinctions—gender, age, illegitimacy, homosexuality, and others. We now ask, too, whether a state may offer certain benefits for pay without providing them gratis to those who cannot pay. Our century has also sought to move equality of opportunity from theory to greater reality, breaking down social, religious, and other barriers to opportunity. But we have also extended the concept of equality from equality of opportunity to include some equality of distribution and less inequality in fact: in addition to the substantial degree of equality now implied in the welfare

---

*The competition between liberty and equality has been seen in terms of economic class: in revolutionary France, we are told, "Liberty was the watchword of the middle-class, equality of the lower."[62] The twentieth-century synthesis, then, perhaps became possible only when and where economic class lines blurred and both classes participated in political power.

conception, in the obligation to accord to every human being an equal minimum of social and economic rights, we have moved to greater "distributive justice" by other programs for "equalization," for narrowing the differences in benefits enjoyed.

The movement in our century, however, has not been all from liberty to equality and welfare. If capitalism has conceded to welfare at least in practice, socialism has conceded to liberty at least in principle.[64] Although socialist theory has yet to be revised to incorporate individual rights in a unified and coherent way, it has ceased to insist on waiting with individual liberty until the masses are liberated and the state withers away. It has found a place for the individual in socialism and has ceased to reject the notion of rights in socialist societies against socialist governments. In Western parliamentary systems, social democrats have come to socialism from democracy; elsewhere, it was urged, one must come to democracy from socialism, but now, not in the end of days. Led by the libertarian socialists of Great Britain and Western Europe, and under pressure of ideological competition with the attractive liberties of the West, socialist theory has accepted, too, the sovereignty of the people (not merely of the proletariat)[65] and popular suffrage. Some Marxists, at least, have accepted the implication of the human rights movement that the human in every individual may predominate over, and have some claims beyond, his class identification. As the human rights movement has moved toward socialist ideas giving full status to economic-social rights, socialism has more readily embraced it, especially since economic-social rights for the individual do in fact tend to depend heavily on economic-social planning and policies for the society as a whole. Socialist governments, then, have promulgated constitutions and included bills of rights, if only in second place to the economic benefits of socialism. Some new socialist states, deriving from Western political inspirations and influences, have put liberty as high as socialism—e.g., Sweden, Israel, and (again, after interruption)

India. Responding to both domestic and international influences, even communist countries have abandoned their rejection of individual rights and, in principle, adhered to the international human rights movement.

The international law of human rights has also synthesized liberty and welfare, more easily, perhaps, since it was building anew. The Universal Declaration of Human Rights and the later covenants included both political-civil and economic-social rights.[66] Equality took special place, not merely the equality implied in that all enjoy a common, equal level of human rights, but equality as a discrete, independent principle rejecting grounds for invidious discriminations that have been common—race, color, sex, religion, political or other opinion, national or social origin, property, birth, or other status.

*   *   *

The second half of the twentieth century has seen essentially universal acceptance of human rights in principle, and general agreement on its content. By universal acceptance, it should be clear, I do not mean that human rights are enjoyed and respected everywhere, or even that all states have a bill or rights that is effective as higher law or have adhered to the international law of human rights. I do not mean that human rights have become assimilated into all cultures, that all men and women everywhere know and enjoy or even aspire to them. I mean only—and find importance in the fact—that philo-osophical as well as political objections to the idea of individual rights have subsided or become irrelevant; indeed, human rights are finding a place in contemporary political, ethical, and moral philosophy, now again preoccupied with "justice," "liberty," and "rights." For natural law today, it is human rights that claim to be the natural, higher law, not the divine right of kings or the sovereignty of the state, not the inferiority of women or races. In positive law today, it is human rights that are national and international law, not the laws of Hitler or some other "jurisprudence of terror." And it is

individual civil-political and economic-social rights that are
accepted as law, not unmitigated collectivism or laissez-faire.
The idea of human rights is accepted in principle by all
governments regardless of other ideology, regardless of
political, economic, or social condition. The universal
acceptance of human rights and of their general content may be
only formal and superficial, without wide agreement, understanding, or even exploration of their philosophical under-
pinnings. Some who accept them stress individualism, and
others condemn individualism as atomism, preferring to stress
fraternity, sociability, and community as the way to individual
dignity and fulfillment. But however formally, however
superficially, however hypocritically even and however deficient the national implementation or international enforcement, no government dares dissent from the ideology of human
rights today.

The conception accepted is that every individual has claims
upon his society—both claims to freedom from undue
governmental intrusion and claims for governmental support
for economic and social welfare. The human rights of the
individual include "self-government," which in complex
modern societies includes a part in "popular sovereignty," in
government and majority rule; such individual participation
and popular sovereignty are not only a fundamental right of
every person but also the foundation and the condition of other
rights. Human rights include an area of autonomy, a core of
freedom from majority rule, from official intrusion even for the
general good. The particular rights implied in this zone of
autonomy are also generally accepted. They include the
political freedoms of speech, press, and assembly; freedom of
thought and conscience; freedom of movement and association; and the right to a fair criminal trial, personal security, and
privacy from government. They include the obligation upon
government to supply basic needs as well—food, shelter,
education, work, and leisure. They prescribe the equal

protection of the laws and forbid invidious discriminations on irrelevant grounds. Although not expressly included in the principal international covenants, some rights to some kind of property clearly are also recognized. International covenants have added such group rights as self-determination and "economic self-determination," that is, every nation's right to control its natural resources. The rights are specific yet flexible enough to be consistent with different political systems, with different degrees and forms of free enterprise as of socialism. They require the opportunity for political participation but do not specify the form or the degree. They neither prescribe nor preclude some inequalities in fact but require at least that level of equality implied in a common minimum of human rights.

Here, then, is the odyssey of an idea to date. Its foundation in the essential, natural autonomy of the individual, governed by social contract with government, has largely given way. Instead, it seeks support today in contemporary values of individual worth and societal need, values that are derived from human psychology and from sociology and that are expressed in positive law, national and international. Popular sovereignty is the accepted source of governmental authority, and popular welfare is the accepted goal of government, although Paine's insistence that "representative government is freedom" is paid off in most countries by periodic plebiscitarianism. The equality of all may be more firmly rooted today in contemporary values than it was as a natural right competing with claims of "natural" inequalities—of race, ethnic groups, religions, gender, rich and poor. Limited watchdog government has given way to activist, interventionist, welfare-promoting government. But the idea of limitations on government, on majorities or elites, in favor of individual rights has taken root. No political system, no political theory now rejects individual rights; all now accept some positive national or international law to protect them, perhaps because we have found ways to mitigate the inconveniences of

TWO

CONSTITUTIONS AND
HUMAN RIGHTS

Human rights are now established in conception and principle and are national and international law for many nations. There is common agreement that every individual has both political-civil and economic-social claims upon his society. But in a world of nation-states, the strength of commitment to human rights and the extent to which it is realized depend on the particular state and its institutions; the condition of human rights thus differs markedly in different societies. Some states, and some groupings of states, are identified by differing ideologies connoting different conceptions and commitments to human rights.

These differences are reflected or signaled in large measure in national constitutions. Constitutions, to be sure, are at best promises, and constitutional promises often remain unfulfilled. But what a constitution promises tells us, at least, what a society pretends or aspires to, where individual rights stand in its political system and scale of values, and much about how rights fare in fact.

In the American conception, a constitution is an instrument that "constitutes" a government and prescribes the blueprint for that government, as the sovereign people of the United States ordained the Constitution of the United States constituting the government described therein. ("The British Constitution" is not in one document but refers to the system of government constituted by historic development and by several acts and documents emanating from recognized authority.) Because it was assumed—especially under theories of popular sovereignty—that the government constituted would be limited, because the U.S. and other constitutions in fact imposed limitations on government, a constitution (and "constitutionalism") came to imply limited government. Because protecting the people's liberties was seen as the principal reason for limitation and because a principal limitation in constitutions was a bill of rights, constitutionalism became identified with respect for individual rights.[1]

Today *constitution* has acquired a more general significance describing a nation's "basic document." There are now constitutions in countries with an ideology antithetical to "constitutionalism," constitutions that do not "constitute" a government, limit its powers, or otherwise protect individual rights. Some countries have used their constitution as a certificate of birth of a nation; as an ideological manifesto; as a description of the system of government that is, perhaps in order to hallow it. But by claiming the title of "constitution" and implicitly pretending to the mantle of constitutionalism, even these national documents cannot be disregarded by governments and are not without significance for human rights.

Ours is the age of constitutions.[2] The first modern constitution was established for the United States nearly two hundred years ago, and for many years it remained one of very few. Today almost every one of 150 states flaunts a constitution. At a time when many nations are being born, a constitution has become a symbol of independence and of becoming a state; in some instances a constitution, including particular safeguards, was necessary to achieve national unity, to assure to minority groups that hesitated to join that they would not be oppressed by the majority. The U.S. Constitution and its Bill of Rights, and its close kin the French Declaration of the Rights of Man, have been models for some constitutions and have influenced many others, directly or through the Universal Declaration on Human Rights, which borrowed from them. But some contemporary constitutions strike a wholly different note, and all of them are different from the eighteenth-century model in major respects. Not every constitution is a social contract between the people and their government. Not every constitution provides for representative government, which Thomas Paine identified with freedom. Not every constitution equally implies "constitutionalism"—effective limits on government in favor of "the people" and of every individual. Not every constitution contains a bill of rights, guarantees or prefers the same rights, means the same thing by the same words, or gives rights effect as law. Not every constitution is equally difficult to abrogate, suspend, or change. Some societies, on the hand, do better than their constitutions promise—for example, the United States, which has supplemented its eighteenth-century constitution by legislation, notably legislation realizing many of the new social and economic rights. A few states in which the condition of human rights is impressive—e.g., Great Britain—do not have constitutions in the accepted sense at all; they have no "higher law," and the protections and benefits the individual enjoys are in principle subject to withdrawal by parliament.*

Since I cannot hope to describe here the condition of rights in every country or even the promises of all their constitutions, I have grouped constitutions, and the political-social-economic

---

*Individual rights were increasingly protected in Great Britain at common law and pursuant to the famous acts beginning with Magna Carta. There was therefore, perhaps, less need to resort to natural law, and no strong pressure to introduce the higher law of a written constitution. In Canada, Australia, and New Zealand, rights were incorporated in controlling acts of the British Parliament. Australia now has a constitution but not a full bill of rights. Canada has adopted a bill of rights by act of parliament, but those rights remain expressly subject to abrogation by future acts of parliament, and parliament can repeal the entire bill at will.[3] In Israel, which also has no constitution, judges have drawn on the British tradition, on natural law, and on the practice of countries with ideologies they identify with (e.g., the United States) to guide them in asserting judicial authority and in interpreting statutes affecting human rights.

systems and the attitudes toward individual rights that they reflect, as democratic-libertarian (Western), socialist-communist, and "other." The first two reflect the major ideological division of our time, and attitudes to human rights have been a principal difference between them. (At the cost of some imbalance, I attempt to describe in particular what the twentieth-century synthesis has done to eighteenth-century rights in the United States.) The "other" category, of course, will catch all the rest. It corresponds substantially to the "Third World," but that is in the main a political-economic grouping and includes some states that for purposes of human rights deserve identification with Western democracy, others with Eastern socialism. For most countries in this category, the lack of any clear ideological identity also speaks to the condition of human rights there.

In looking at constitutionalism in different societies and different kinds of societies, I look for reflections on human rights as now conceived, both political-civil and economic-social rights for individuals. I do not consider the overarching ideological conflict between socialism and capitalism as it relates to human rights: whether capitalism or socialism (or their approximations) are themselves consistent with or conducive to human rights. Socialists might see even in contemporary Western "mixed economies" all the contradictions of capitalism—inefficiency in the use of resources, including human resources; powerful selfish interests dictating national policy at home and abroad; gross inequalities in income and wealth, therefore in economic power, and consequently in political power and in meaningful freedom; the encouragement of confrontation and competition rather than cooperation. Critics of socialism, on the other hand, point to the subordination of the individual and of human values to the ends of the state; the lack of economic freedom; the tendency to authoritarianism, a one party-state, and the elimination of opposition and political freedom; the power of bureaucracy and political elites creating their own inequalities. But both socialist and capitalist states, and more or less socialist and more or less capitalist states, have accepted the rights and the conception of rights articulated in the Universal Declaration, and we may appropriately consider how these rights are reflected in their constitutional systems.

Constitutional Rights in Democratic-Libertarian Countries

Almost all countries now declare sovereignty to be in "the people" and describe themselves as democracies. Only a small number of them are democracies "Western style"—the United States, Great Britain and its "Old Commonwealth" offspring, the countries of Western Europe (including perhaps Portugal and Spain, since 1976), some in Latin America (although which ones at which times is sometimes debatable), and a few elsewhere. Since their claim to democracy, to represent authentic rule by all the people, is challenged (notably by communism) and since, strictly, "democracy" (rule by the people) satisfies a human right to self-government but does not imply other rights for the individual against "the government by the people," these countries might be described as "representative-libertarian." They are characterized by commitment to a representative government with regular, effective universal suffrage, as well as to individual freedom from too much government even by the people's representatives. Although representative government as well as individual freedom reflect respect for the individual, they may diverge in tension when the individual asserts rights against the majority, when he appeals to a higher natural or ancestral law, to the society's "deeper instincts" (rather than the majority's present predilections).[4]

The United States

American constitutionalism found its original, authentic expression not in the U.S. Constitution but in the earlier state constitutions, notably the Virginia Declaration of Rights

(1776) and the Massachusetts Constitution of 1780.[5] Unlike these, the U.S. Constitution was not originally a full-blown expression of constitutionalism, limited government, and respect for individual rights. That is in large measure because historically and conceptually the Constitution descended from the Articles of Confederation, which did not establish a "government" but only a league of states, which dealt only with union and did not, therefore, concern themselves with philosophy of government or with the relation between the individual and society. Although the framers of the U.S. Constitution converted the league of states into a federal government, a philosophy of limited government and individual rights is only lightly implied. That philosophy was supplied in part by the Bill of Rights and later amendments; some was also added later by constitutional interpretation in the light of the constitutionalism believed to be our heritage, as reflected in the Declaration and early state constitutions.[6] (I shall simplify here by concentrating on the federal government and the federal Constitution, but what I say about human rights generally applies also to state constitutions, and to individual rights vis-à-vis state governments, to which the federal Constitution spoke little until after the Civil War but which are now essentially governed by it and by federal law and institutions.)

The United States is not necessarily the principal or the prototypical libertarian democracy, but it has well-developed human rights doctrines and institutions for protecting them. Building on eighteenth-century fundamentals—popular sovereignty, limited government, and retained individual rights— the United States has offered several elements to contemporary human rights ideology:

- a written constitution, difficult to abrogate, replace, suspend, or change
- the Constitution as the source of governmental authority and the condition of its legitimacy

- safeguards against too-strong government by separation of powers, checks and balances, federalism
- representative government as a basic right
- a bill of political-civil rights
- both the constitutional blueprint of government and the bill of rights authoritatively interpreted and maintained by an independent judiciary whose mandate is conclusive

Each of these elements has contributed to the growth of human rights in the United States, and all are reflected in their present condition. The written constitution helped maintain the limitations on federal and state governments and on their particular branches, and promoted the judicial role as constitutional arbiter. The Constitution has not been abrogated or replaced, and amendments have been few;* and no constitutional amendment has detracted from the Bill of Rights or reduced the limitations on government resulting from the separation of powers. The Civil War amendments brought radical change in our federalism. Indeed, some might see them as so modifying the character of government as to effect a new constitution, but they also enhanced the content of human rights and extended the means for protecting them. They abolished slavery, ordained the equal protection of the laws for all, and laid the groundwork for protecting other human rights against state infringement by effectively placing all human rights under federal scrutiny and protection. Later amendments also enhanced rather than diminished human

---

*The Bill of Rights, although it was appended by amendment, is properly seen as part of the "original package" since it was a condition of ratification in some of the states. Of the other sixteen amendments (in nearly 200 years) two (the Eighteenth and the Twenty-first) largely canceled each other. Most of the others, too, now seem of minor significance, surely as regards individual rights. One (XXIV)—invalidating the poll tax—anticipated what was about to happen by judicial interpretation of the Constitution.[7] Others may also have been unnecessary; even the purpose of the amendment eliminating sex discrimination in voting (XIX) might in time have been achieved under the equal protection clause of the Fourteenth Amendment.

rights. Though not apparently dealing with human rights, the Sixteenth Amendment, which authorizes the progressive income tax, reflects a philosophy of distributing burdens of citizenship in relation to capacity; it was probably indispensable to provide the money that made possible the transformation of the United States into a welfare state responding to economic and social rights. The Seventeenth Amendment, which provides for the direct election of senators, improved the individual's right to participate in his government; the Nineteenth provided that the right to vote shall not be denied on account of sex.

The genius and prescience of the framers, the availability of the judiciary to adapt and develop the general principles of the Constitution and to arbitrate political controversy—as well, no doubt, as great good fortune—have saved the United States from more frequent and more radical change. These have saved us, too, from extraconstitutional government, and from emergency suspensions of the Constitution or of particular rights, both of which have bedeviled human rights in other countries. The Constitution does not provide for its own suspension, and that has never been attempted, even in time of war. Only the privilege of the writ of habeas corpus can be suspended, only by Congress, only in case of rebellion or invasion, and then only if the public safety requires it (Article I, section 9). It was suspended during the Civil War, and other rights have been curtailed then and during later wars: the relocation of Americans of Japanese ancestry during World War II was an inglorious chapter, held by the courts to be constitutionally permissible. But we have not otherwise had mass detentions or other major derogations from rights.[8]

That separation of powers and federalism help preserve individual rights by preventing concentration of governmental power has been an article of faith, difficult to test. After nearly 200 years, although the branches of government and relations among them are transformed, separation and checks and balances survive in principle and largely in fact. Presidential

power has expanded greatly from our constitutional beginnings and has known periods of extravagant growth, especially
during the Civil War, the New Deal years, World War II, and
since; it has sometimes been exercised with particular
deleterious effect on individual rights—recently, for example,
by wiretapping, allegedly to protect national security. But
particular excesses have been ended by the courts,[9] and
imbalances are periodically restored or rectified, as when
Congress legislated to control the president's resort to the use of
force abroad, or to make international agreements, on his own
authority.[10] The courts have also protected the president's
power from congressional invasion, for example, his power to
appoint officials.[11] Some ask whether our ancestors' fear of the
concentration of power remains justified, whether a bill of
rights effectively administered by the judiciary is not a
sufficient safeguard making separation of political power less
necessary and its ineffectiveness too costly.[12] But the case of
Richard Nixon and the role of Congress in his downfall have
restored faith in the importance of that separation.

Federalism as a limitation on too-strong government seems
hardly to matter today, for in constitutional principle, federal
power is nearly unlimited[13] (although it cannot interfere with
the ability of the states to function as independent governments
in their local domains).[14] But if we remain a federal state largely
by legislative grace, Congress is highly sensitive to powerful
centrifugal, forces that resist concentration of governmental
power.[15] On the other hand, the growth of federal power has
unleashed national forces pressing for positive action to
promote and protect individual rights. It has increased the
security of individual rights against invasion by the states and
inexorably also against invasion by the federal government.

Representative government was a cardinal principle of the
American Revolution, but its realization in the Constitution
was blurred by indirect election of the president and of senators
and by limited suffrage. Now the Senate, like the House of
Representatives, is elected directly, and the election of the

president by the Electoral College has been reduced to formality and made more responsible to popular suffrage (although along state rather than national lines). More directly, the right to participate in self-government has matured as suffrage has become a virtually universal right for all citizens, as citizenship has become easy to acquire, as other voting qualifications have been eliminated, and as invidious obstacles to voting (e.g., racial discrimination) have been strongly combated.[16] The Constitution has been held also to require substantial equality in voting power, "one man, one vote."[17]

Judicial review is the unique U.S. contribution to constitutionalism, and individual rights are now its principal beneficiary.* What the founding fathers did not make explicit, what Chief Justice Marshall seemed to assert only in limited conception and narrow compass, is now firmly established and broadly conceived: the courts are the authoritative, supreme, and final arbiters of constitutional rights, and government, federal as well as state, legislative as well as executive, does not flout or challenge them.[19]

Rights in the United States have developed from the eighteenth-century ideas I have noted.[20] Indeed, because—except for the addition of "the equal protection of the laws" in the Fourteenth Amendment—we still use the same words with which we began, because our Bill of Rights has not been formally amended, it is easy for us to forget the limited conception of individual rights we had early and to overlook recent change and growth.

Originally, our declared rights were essentially political. The system of government established by the Constitution, and the bill of rights appended thereto, were designed primarily to protect "the people"—the effective, propertied, voting citizenry—from tyranny and repression; it is not indisputable that

---

*Issues of federalism and separation of powers, once the staple of constitutional adjudication, provide the courts with little business today. Only state regulation and taxation of interstate commerce continue to throw up living federalism issues.[18]

they reflected care for the dignity and autonomy of the individual human being, and of all human beings equally. (It has been said they protected not the rights of man, but the rights of gentlemen.) The freedoms we put in first place—speech, press, assembly—were seen primarily as political liberties with political purposes, to safeguard representative government as then conceived; that they sought to safeguard individual "self-expression" generally, or even radical political heresy, is open to question.[21] Even the freedom of religion probably reflected a concern to provide political protection for religious dissenters and to avoid religious hostility as much as it reflected concern for individual conscience. The "right of the people to be secure," the rule of law implied in "due process of law," the protection of property against confiscation, the catalog of rights for those who might be accused of crime, although couched as rights of every person, also seem to reflect a desire to safeguard the established respectable citizenry against various known forms of repression by tyrannical governments—rather than tenderness and respect for individual man, even the least worthy and the criminal. There was, I have noted, no freedom from slavery, no guarantee of equality, no universal suffrage.

We have come a long way, under the same words, by a complicated process that still goes on, but the development of our human rights has hardly been progressive and linear. For almost a hundred years, our rights remained largely what they had been as the country expanded geographically and economically and struggled with the terrible burden of slavery. Surely on the national level, but even within the states (which governed individuals directly every day) our conception of rights did not change nor our enjoyment of them grow appreciably. The states were not bound by the Bill of Rights in the U.S. Constitution, but only by what was in their own constitutions, as interpreted and enforced by their own institutions.[22] Of the few clauses in the original U.S. Constitution that limited state invasions of private rights, only that forbidding the impairment of contracts was "active" in the

Supreme Court before the Civil War, and it was utilized largely to protect associations and substantial landholders.[23] The only act of Congress invalidated before the Civil War was the Missouri Compromise, inter alia because it deprived Dred Scott's master of his property without due process of law.[24]

Major change came with the "peace treaty" ending the Civil War, i.e., with the Thirteenth, Fourteenth, and Fifteenth amendments. These, too, were probably not designed to realize radical advances in human rights generally, only to abolish slavery (as some of our states and other countries had done earlier) and the disabilities and other "badges" of slavery. The Civil War amendments had immediate importance of a different order, for they nationalized individual rights, subjecting the actions of the states—of the northern victors as of the vanquished South—to Federal constitutional limitations, to scrutiny by the federal judiciary, and to congressional regulation. And they planted in the Constitution (some think unwittingly) seeds that later flourished in luxuriant conceptions of equality, liberty, due process of law, and citizenship that cannot be taken away against the individual's wish.[25]

Although the original rights were generally respected, for more than a half-century after the Civil War the courts were not the champions of rights we have come to think them to be; indeed, in important respects, their constitutional readings prevented the promotion of human rights both by Congress and by progressive states. Their narrow readings of the Fourteenth Amendment, including one limiting its prohibitions to "state action" narrowly conceived (not to private action), invalidated much of what Congress had done in the aftermath of the Civil War.[26] Later, narrow judicial construction of other constitutional grants of power to Congress invalidated the progressive income tax (on which governmental support for economic-social rights now heavily depends), efforts to close interstate commerce to the products of child labor, and efforts to regulate wages and hours and other labor conditions.[27] It is ironical that the courts also invoked individual rights doctrine to prevent both federal and state action to promote individual welfare, and slowed down the slow move of the United States toward the welfare state for half a century: regulation of wages, hours, and labor relations were held to be inappropriate purposes of government, deprivations of property, and infringements of liberty of contract.[28] Equality, too, suffered, as the courts accepted segregation and other traditional, "natural" inequalities, upholding, for example, the authority of the state to exclude women from the practice of law.[29] Narrow readings of the Bill of Rights led the courts to accept limitations on freedom of speech during and after World War I[30] and other restrictions on rights and liberties: for forty years, for example, wiretapping was held not a form of search and seizure subject to the limitations of the Fourth Amendment.[31]

The rapid growth of human rights in the United States came with the New Deal and World War II. I cannot here describe the particular steps, but the results to date are impressive. The Fourteenth Amendment was held to have incorporated, and rendered applicable to the states, the principal provisions of the Bill of Rights—freedom of speech, press, assembly, religion, the security of the home and the person, safeguards for those accused of crime.* Incorporation also "homogenized" rights against the federal and state governments, rendering them essentially the same in every state as they were against the increasingly interventionist federal government.

Even more impressive has been the expansion of our eighteenth-century rights in conception and content. We have opened our Constitution to every man and woman, to the least and the worst of them. We have opened it also to new rights and to expanded conceptions of old rights. We have moved beyond political rights to civil and personal rights, rooted in

----

*In principle the Bill of Rights is incorporated only selectively, but apparently all of its "living" provisions (I exclude the Second and Third amendments—the right to bear arms and not to quarter troops) are incorporated except the right to indictment by a grand jury, and to jury trial in civil cases.[32] Even the "right to privacy" was first found in the "penumbra" of various provisions of the Bill of Rights, and held to be incorporated.[33]

conceptions of essential individual dignity and worth. We safeguard not only political freedom but also, in principle, social, sexual, and other personal freedom, privacy, autonomy, idiosyncrasy.[34] Freedom of speech and press now protects not only political and religious, but also economic, speech, and publication, e.g., labor picketing and commercial advertising and "self-expression" against censors of morals.[35] Speech is protected even when it is "symbolic," as in wearing an arm band to protest a war or in refusing to salute the flag;[36] even one's money may talk, as by contributions to political campaigns, without ready limits.[37] The press, too, enjoys freedom extending far beyond its relevance to the political process and is now associated with the reader's "right to know." It was not enjoined from publishing confidential official documents, and its rights outweighed also the right of a "public" (not necessarily political) individual to be free from libel or private persons' rights to privacy.[38] Freedom of speech and press includes a right of access to a public forum; it also includes the freedom not to speak or publish, to speak and publish anonymously, to be free of governmental inquiry into what one thinks and says.[39] Out of these rights and the right of assembly we have made a right of association,* of anonymous association, of nonassociation.[40] Freedom of religion means not only that there must be no interference with, but also no burden on, the free exercise of religion: the state may not deny unemployment benefits to one who cannot obtain employment because she is a Sabbatarian.[41] The prohibition on establishing religion means a wall of separation between church and state,

---

*For the individual, identification and association with a group—for example, an ethnic, religious, or linguistic identification, as for blacks, Chicanos, Jews—may not only be an important right, but may also be necessary in order for the individual to achieve and assure minimum individual dignity and the protection of other rights. The group may also have its own rights that are more or less than, but different from, the sum of the rights of the individuals who constitute it, although focus on the rights of the group sometimes dilutes concern for individual rights against the group or against the larger society.

and neither the federal nor the state governments may ɡ
financial aid to religious institutions or permit Bible reading
or prayer in public schools.[42] Freedom from unreasonable
search and seizure applies not only to the home but also to the
office and the automobile; not only to physical but also to
technological intrusion, e.g., wiretapping;[43] not only to
incursions by the police but also to visits by health and fire
inspectors.[44]

Perhaps the greatest expansion has been in the rights of those
accused of crime. For them, the Bill of Rights, its principal
provisions incorporated in the Fourteenth Amendment and
applicable also to the states, is now a broader conception: not
only does it protect the respectable and innocent against the
governmental oppressor, but even criminals have rights—to a
fair trial (without improperly obtained evidence), to counsel
(provided by the government if the defendant cannot provide
his own), to freedom from self-incrimination and from
comment on his failure to testify.[45] Penological assumptions
and practices have acquired a constitutional dimension. A
person cannot be punished for a condition—intoxication, the
influence of drugs—that he was unable to resist; punishment
that is excessive in relation to the crime is forbidden as "cruel
and unusual," and the death penalty, in particular, may not be
imposed to protect values other than life, e.g., for rape.[46] Some
have questioned the constitutionality of punishment that is
retributive rather than preventive, deterrent, or rehabilitative.[47]
And for some Supreme Court justices (though not, it proved,
for a majority), capital punishment became unconstitutional
because it was cruel and unusual, or because it was being meted
out erratically, capriciously, with racial or social discrimination.[48]

The equal protection of the laws has also acquired new
ramifications (including the right to equal voting power),[49]
and by the interpretation of the due process clause of the Fifth
Amendment, the Constitution now effectively requires of the
federal government the same equal protection of the laws that

the Fourteenth Amendment expressly imposed on the states.[50] All racial classifications are suspect and sharply scrutinized, and invidious discrimination on account of race, "whether accomplished ingeniously or ingenuously," is readily rejected.[51] Official separation of the races, even "separate but equal," is outlawed.[52] There has been a fundamental and, I believe, irreversible transformation in the status of women. In law, discriminations against women, reflecting stereotyped generalizations and outdated sociological assumptions, no longer seem "natural" and inevitable and are invalid; and the new equality of the genders entitles men also to freedom from irrational discrimination.[53] The poor, too, have rights to equal protection, and the state cannot offer important rights—a criminal appeal, a divorce—for pay without making them available gratis to those who cannot pay.[54] Other once-axiomatic inequalities are no longer acceptable: the state cannot deny welfare benefits, public employment, admission to the professions to aliens;[55] it cannot maintain irrelevant distinctions between legitimate and illegitimate children.[56] Other once-closed categories are open: prisoners now have rights, as do military personnel, mental patients, pupils in the schools, and children independently of their parents.[57]

The courts also found new rights, for example, a right to travel, abroad as well as interstate; and they have invalidated local residence requirements as a condition of enjoying rights or benefits because such requirements discouraged interstate travel.[58] In what can be seen as a reversion to eighteenth-century principle, the courts have found an area of fundamental individual autonomy (called "privacy"), invasions of which will be sharply scrutinized and invalidated unless they serve a compelling state interest. Hence, the state may not forbid the use of contraceptives, or abortion in the first trimester of pregnancy, or indulging oneself with obscene materials in private.[59] Parents may send their children to private schools, and Amish parents may even refuse to send their children to high school at all when that would contravene their scruples.[60] On the horizon may be rights undreamed of—a right to be born and a right to die; rights for the dead and the unborn; rights to security, peace, a healthy environment; rights for the environment, the animal, even the vegetable and mineral.[61]

The explosion of rights I have described promises even more, for it confirms the essentially open character of our Constitution, as always subject to present synthesis of eternal, immutable principle with contemporary values both home-grown and imported. Old assumptions are reexamined, stereotypes are penetrated, and rights are accepted today that were not conceived a decade ago. Old laws and accepted official practices, and legislative delegations lending themselves to official abuse, are no longer tolerated: e.g., crimes such as loitering or vagrancy are now void for vagueness, because the activities are essentially inoffensive and give too much power and discretion to officials, too little warning to the putative offender. Overbroad laws are invalidated or narrowed to prevent them from "chilling" and discouraging the exercise of important freedoms.[62]

Perhaps the inevitable consequence of expanding and proliferating rights was the clear emergence of the principle of "balancing" individual liberty and public interest to determine the limits of each. Although the courts do not now attend seriously to objections that economic and social regulation limits individual autonomy or liberty, in principle all governmental action must still justify itself as a means rationally linked to some public purpose.[63] But rights are not absolute, and virtually every right might in some times and circumstances give way to some other public good. Some individual rights and freedoms, however—speech, press, assembly, religion, old and new privacy, freedom from racial discrimination—are fundamental, preferred; invasions are suspect and will be sharply scrutinized and will be sustained only for a compelling state interest (although the Supreme Court has not done well in justifying the weights it gives to particular rights and has done nothing at all to explain the weights assigned to different public interests.)[64] The courts also balance conflicting rights—for example, the freedom of the press and the privacy of the individual or fair trial for the accused—again in scales of their own device, scales that reflect society's human rights values as they see them.[65]

I have been discussing the rights Americans now have as higher law, regardless of the will of majorities and of their representatives and officials. But the courts have now unleashed and even encouraged Congress and state legislatures to expand individual rights. The extension of federal power, notably the commerce power, has enabled Congress to legislate against private discriminations (e.g., on account of race) and other private infringements.[66] (Such legislation, of course, in effect denies persons a "right" to discriminate, to be caprious or unjust.) Expansive interpretations of the Civil War amendments have permitted sophisticated legislation to protect the right to vote and the exercise of other rights free from official or private interference.[67] And imaginative lawyers and sympathetic courts have found that even old civil rights acts give protections against invasions of newly conceived rights, and that they likewise give new remedies, for example, a prohibition on private discrimination in the sale or rental of housing or in admission to private school, or money damages against police who commit unreasonable search or seizure.[68]

Congress has also created the "right to know" by "freedom of information" acts.[69] It has extended the right of conscientious objection to military service.[70] It has created rights to a healthier environment.[71] Federal example has encouraged emulation by the states, and some states have taken such rights further.[72]

Perhaps the most significant legislative extension of rights has been that which, beginning some forty years ago, brought economic and social "rights" to Americans. These rights did not come easily. The United States has become a welfare state not by constitutional imperative or encouragement but, indeed, over strong constitutional resistance. Welfare government had to overcome resistance to governmental intervention and activism, resistance that flew the flag of individual autonomy and limited conceptions of government; resistance to various economic regulations, flying the flag of economic liberty; resistance to strong federal government, flying the flag of states' rights; resistance to massive government spending based on heavy progressive taxation, flying flags of property, liberty and equality.[73] Except for public education provided by the states early, the welfare state began slowly in the United States, with regulation of public utilities that enjoyed official monopoly and with antitrust laws seen as necessary to keep the market free and make laissez-faire work. A constitutional amendment was required to institute the progressive income tax. Only after deep economic depression came intensive regulation of business and labor relations, minimum wages and maximum hours, social security, expanding government employment and government work programs—and constitutional reinterpretations to make them acceptable. A second world war and decades of technological, political, and social change, and ideas and example from abroad have proliferated welfare programs and magnified them manyfold. Economic and social benefits, of course, establish equal entitlement as regards minimum basic needs; they have even moved our society a few steps from merely equal protection of the laws and equal opportunity to less inequality and more just distribution in fact. Today, it might even be claimed that the United States is substantially committed to that principle of foreign origin, "from each according to his ability, to each according to his need."[74]

The rights of man in the United States, it need hardly be said, are far from perfect. Our past sins are grievous and notorious: genocide and lesser violations of the Indian; slavery, racial segregation, and other badges of slavery for blacks; other racial, ethnic, and religious discriminations, including relocations and concentrations of citizens of Japanese ancestry in time of war; Chinese exclusion and other racist immigration laws; postwar anticommunist hunts also invading and chilling political freedoms of others, and many more.

If these are for the largest part happily past, other offenses are still with us. There are still racial discriminations and inequalities, at least de facto, and debatable acceptance of private discrimination.[75] Our valued freedoms are sometimes empty for those unable or afraid to exercise them, or denied access to media that will make them effective or competitive. There is poverty, unemployment (which falls particularly heavily on blacks and other minorities), inadequate housing and health care, even hunger, and there are wider economic inequities and inequalities. Our immigration, exclusion, and deportation laws are built on outdated conceptions, for example, on the absolute right of Congress to exclude and deport.[76] Some object to balancing away rights in principle, or to the balance struck in particular instances, say, the preference of the right to know over the right of privacy.[77] Some see violations of rights in the remaining laws against obscenity, in limitations on newspapers and newspapermen, in regulation of other communications media; some have objected to tolerating laws against group libel.[78] Some see retrogression in "affirmative action," discriminating in favor of the once-oppressed to the disadvantage of others.[79] Some see failures of rights in excessive toleration, in respecting freedom for those who abuse it, in too much "legalism" at the expense of order, in failing generally to provide freedom from fear. Even where our principles are unexceptionable, there are ever-present instances where practice deviates from principle and is not readily remedied: there have been accusations and some evidence of "political justice"—denial of due process and equal protection to communists and "leftists," Black Panthers, longhairs, the deviant, the stranger. Police abuses are too frequent and notorious, and governmental technology threatens essential privacy.

But in all, I conclude, human rights—civil-political as well as economic-social—are alive and rather well in the United States.

Other Libertarian Democracies

I cannot pretend to describe even the constitutions and laws—surely not the condition of human rights—in other liberal democracies in detail. We know enough of their constitutions, laws, and institutions, and something of their practices, however, to confirm that the condition of human rights in those countries is in principle and in general not too different from what it is in the United States. These liberal democracies accord decent respect to similar rights and freedoms, and to the equal protection of the laws and equality of opportunity. They provide social services and "welfare."

There are, I stress, substantial differences among these democracies. Americans tend to see their way of doing things as "the human rights way"; and yet, of the elements the United States has contributed to the theology and institutionalization of human rights, one or more are absent in other Western democracies. We pride ourselves on a written constitution, but Great Britain does not have any in the same sense. (There have been strong suggestions by eminent persons that Great Britain should consider an authentic bill of rights having status as superior law.)[80] The United States Constitution is difficult to replace or amend, but France has replaced its constitution and radically changed its form of government several times. The constitution or particular fundamental rights have periodically been suspended even in the more libertarian of Latin American countries.[81] The United States has a presidential system, separation of powers, and abiding federalism; there is no federalism in most countries of Western Europe, the French presidential system is different from ours, and parliamentary systems have no meaningful separation of powers: if individual rights depend on such diffusion of power, they would seem to be ever in jeopardy where power is effectively in the hands of a prime minister and cabinet with party discipline disarming his majority in parliament. The U.S. hallmark is judicial review to protect individual rights against both legislative and executive violation, but judicial review can protect human rights only to the extent to which the higher law of a constitution guarantees them. In Great Britain, there is no higher law, Parliament is supreme and in principle unlimited (and cannot render itself limited); individuals cannot have rights against Parliament, and there can be no judicial review of its acts for alleged violations of individual rights.* Even where constitutions and judicial review have long existed, as in several countries in Latin America, or have recently come (France, Germany, Italy), the scope of judicial review is apparently narrower and its significance for human rights less in varying degrees than in the United States.[83]

The United States and some other Western democracies also differ in their conceptions of rights and in the rights they prize and prefer. In the United States, rights are against government and are protected against invasion by government; in some countries, they are conceived as having independent status, to be protected also against invasion by private persons.[84] The United States goes farther than others in preferring freedom of speech and press—even when they encourage racial hatred or international tension or even war. We prefer the right to know; others prefer the right of privacy, the right not to be published about. France and Germany are apparently more sensitive to governmental intrusions on privacy, to "bugging" and governmental collection of data about individuals. We favor the right of the mother to abort and not bear a child; others prefer a right for the foetus to live.[85] There is an established

*It has been argued that in Great Britain "parliamentary supremacy" implies only that it is supreme over the monarchy, but does not mean that its acts cannot be invalidated by the courts. If so, the courts would be asserting some higher, natural "common law"; it would be difficult for a court to invalidate an act of Parliament because it violated provisions of "the British Constitution" as contained in acts of earlier parliaments, without finding some basis for giving the earlier acts higher status. The accepted view is that in fact the courts have no authority to review and invalidate acts of Parliament, although they may attempt to construe them to avoid conflict with major acts of earlier parliaments.[82]

church in England, Denmark, and other countries, and even where there is not, relations between church and state look quite different from our stark separation. As regards the rights of those accused of crime, our system is accusatorial and adversary, that of some others is inquisitorial; some provide no jury trial, have no privilege against self-incrimination, do not exclude unlawfully obtained probative evidence (which in the United States often frees the guilty in order to discipline the police). There are important differences between the United States and Great Britain or France in their willingness to impinge on freedom of the press to protect fair trial. Western democracies differ also in their willingness to infringe on individual autonomy to achieve greater equality or more welfare rights. The United States differs from other countries, too, in the circumstances in which, in the means by which, in the purposes for which, rights may be suspended or abridged: our "balancing" of rights and public interest does not come out at the same place as, say, French applications of the requirements of *ordre public*. We have been largely abandoning, while some other Western countries retain, limitations on freedom in behalf of "public morals." (Even in the United States, moreover, citizens—and Supreme Court justices—are not unanimous that prevailing doctrine is "correct" as to what the Constitution requires or should require.)

In all these countries, however, the established political-civil rights and liberties are commonly protected. They are legal rights, spelled out in detail in statute if not in constitution, and they are not in fact easy to change. Emergency provisions permitting derogation from rights are limited, carefully defined, procedurally safeguarded, infrequently invoked; preventive detention and official torture are unusual and unacceptable.[86] There is essential equality under law, and equal opportunity, as well as some tendencies to equalize and distribute wealth more justly. They provide social services and welfare. There is individual choice of profession, occupation, and location of work and residence; it is free of governmental compulsion. Although there is also official planning, extensive governmental intervention in the economy, and a commitment to the welfare state, all these countries have, and seem to consider to be a form of liberty, a substantial measure of "modified capitalism" and of freedom of enterprise.

What do Western democratic-libertarian countries have in common that might explain common human rights principles, commitments, and practices? In their institutions, laws, and traditions, there is emphasis on the essential autonomy, dignity, and value of the individual. Although all these states are now "socialist" in some measure, there is a basic reluctance to sacrifice the individual even for the greater good of all (except in exceptional, temporary, "vital," and traditional contexts, such as war or major emergency.)* Although all states now "plan," there is a deep reluctance to sacrifice the present to the future, to sacrifice important rights of living persons for uncertain benefits to uncertain generations to come.

As societies, they are politically, economically, and socially developed and stable,** and by tradition and by other influences, they are "open societies." Government is representative, there is political opposition and more than one party, and suffrage is essentially universal. Government is responsible and accountable to the people, and enough of the people are politically aware to make that accountability meaningful. The judiciary is independent, and justice is largely apolitical. There is concern for human rights by citizenry, and sensitivity to them by officials. There is a free press alert to violations of human rights, and there are institutions for vindicating them.

---

*Even in war, no particular individual is chosen to be sacrificed; all are in principle equally liable to "the strange arithmetic of chance." Indeed, a lower federal court held it a violation of the equal protection of the laws to conscript men but not women, but that decision was later reversed.[87]

**Compare a recent study that relates the effectiveness of judicial review in different countries in Latin America to levels of economic development.[88]

Some of these qualities I have catalogued may be the result of respect for human rights, rather than cause of it; some may be fortuitous and irrelevant; some may be alternative paths to human rights, others cumulative; surely some matter more than others, singly or in combination. Some of these characteristics may change, from internal or international causes, and we might see whether the condition of human rights is modified in consequence.

The future of human rights in today's libertarian democracies cannot be taken for granted. Each of these countries has human rights problems today. Some question the depth of commitment to human rights in countries where there was repression not too long ago, for example, in Portugal or Spain, perhaps even in Germany and Italy. Some fear communism in France or Italy and speculate as to whether that would make them, as regards human rights, more like socialist Sweden, or more like Hungary, or different from either. A while ago some feared that economic collapse might erode human rights even in Great Britain—the mother, or grandmother, of human rights. But whether, to what extent, and in what form human rights survive in these countries will, I believe, depend principally on what happens to those societal qualities, institutions, and attitudes I have described. While these essentially survive, there is reason to be confident. They will also be influenced, for better and for worse, by what happens to human rights in other countries, and by other external and international influences.

Socialist-Communist Constitutions and Human Rights

"Socialism" has more or less precise philosophical and historical connotations, but politically and popularly it is often used loosely to describe a variety of societies. They have in common, as the term may imply, an aspiration to maximize the economic-social welfare of all. They tend to have official economic planning; public ownership of public utilities, of other principal industries, and financial institutions ("the means of production"); and limitations on individual economic enterprise and on accumulation of private property.

For our purposes, surely, "socialism" is not to be contrasted with "democracy," for they respond to different questions about society.* Strictly, democracy (and representative government) imply only "rule by the people," and the people might wish to pursue socialism.** Moreover, socialism is not necessarily inconsistent with substantial individual freedom, for, in principle, a socialist society might favor large freedom (in matters other than economic organization and activity), and, indeed, the better distribution of economic justice may make such freedoms more meaningful for all.[89] There have been libertarian socialists and, for periods, libertarian near-socialist governments in Great Britain, Western Europe, and elsewhere; Sweden, Israel, and (again) India, for example, have been hailed as countries where both human rights and socialism flourish.[90]

Socialist societies do, however, differ from the Western democracies at least in perspective and emphasis. The latter still have a bias toward individual freedom, implying limitations on government, but socialism puts the society foremost, limits individual autonomy for the benefit of the group, and does not favor limitations on a socialist government's freedom to act for the common benefit even at substantial expense to some individuals. Strictly, too, Western democracy may imply substantial freedom of economic enterprise and freedom from the degree of regulation and

---

*"National socialism" (Nazism), most would insist, usurped the socialist label. It had in common with other socialisms planning and regulation for the benefit of the "state," with the individual submerged. But German national-socialism was not "for export" as universal, was not egalitarian (even for all the members of the national society), and not benign, either domestically or toward neighboring societies. Government and leadership were not representative of or accountable to the people. Submergence of the individual was not temporary, even in theory.

**In some of today's socialist states, however, the people's right to abandon socialism seems excluded.

planning associated with socialism. Freedom of enterprise tends also to be associated with opportunity to earn greater rewards, but socialism elevates equality, in distribution and enjoyment, with greater rewards perhaps for those who contribute more to the socialist good.

In principle, then, there might be socialism with or without democracy, and with less or more individual autonomy and liberty. Here, however, I consider Marxist-Leninist socialism, the ideology that has offered itself as an alternative to Western democracy including its emphasis on individual rights. Namely, I consider Marxist-Leninist socialism as realized in the largest, most populous socialist (communist) states—the Soviet Union and the People's Republic of China—with a postscript for Castro's Cuba. (In the Chinese constitution of 1978, Marxism-Leninism is coupled with Mao Tse-tung's thought as "the guiding ideology of the People's Republic of China.")[91] Again, I am concerned here not with the changing conditions of human rights in these and other communist countries in fact, but with communism in principle, with the constitutions the communist states have promulgated, with their aspirations, protestations, and promises, and with what these signify for human rights.

Marxist-Leninist principle had no place or use for individual rights: rights were egoistic and favored private interests and private desires separated from the community. They were perhaps desirable for workers in capitalist societies and might help bring about socialism, but they in principle were profoundly insufficient, a bourgeois illusion. For Marxist-Leninist socialism, individualism in all its forms was antisocialist: there could be no individual rights against a socialist state and government; the individual had duties to society, not rights against it, though he enjoyed rights (benefits) as part of the group. Individual freedoms could be tolerated only as they contributed to, or at least did not hinder, the development of socialism. When the state withered away, the individual would be wholly free, but until that happened,

socialist government could not be limited by any notion of
individual rights, for such limitations would interfere with the
full realization of socialism.[92]

In recent decades, Marxist-Leninist (Stalinist-Marxist)
theory has had to respond to a changed world. Under pressure
from Western ideas of freedom that are widely disseminated
and have great popular appeal and from an international
human rights movement with growing political importance,
the USSR, at least, has been impelled to adopt the rhetoric of
individual rights,. join the international human rights
movement, and assume international human rights obligations by adhering to international agreements.[93] Soviet
theorists have apparently not yet incorporated that development into contemporary communist theory, but communist
societies have had to adjust to the human rights ideology,
which is now reflected in communist law and institutions,
including the new Soviet constitution of 1977 and the Chinese
constitution of 1978.

There are large similarities in doctrine and in the condition
of human rights in the Soviet Union and communist China;
there are also significant differences between them, even in
doctrine, surely in practice. It is not obvious which elements—
of similarity or of difference—are ideological and which are
"national." It is not obvious which differences, appearing even
in the respective constitutions, reflect the difference in the birth
date of the two revolutions, or the age of the two socialist
societies, and which bespeak historic, geographical, sociological, economic, political, or other differences between
Russia and China.[94] It is not easy to determine what is
temporary, what is intrinsic. To some extent differences in
dogma, at least, seem clearly ideological and adversary. The
1954 constitution of the People's Republic of China followed
the 1936 Soviet constitution closely, but intervening divergence
and hostility caused China, in the 1975 constitution, to reject
Soviet "deviations" and to reassert revolutionary dedication
and ideological purity. (The 1975 constitution also eliminated

a paragraph proclaiming friendship for the USSR and the people's democracies.) The 1978 constitution, however, moved back some way toward the earlier model, also in respects relevant to human rights.

The constitutions of the Soviet Union and China are not Thomas Paine's constitutions. They were not ordained and established by the people as the contract with, and the condition of, the government they established. The constitution is not "a thing antecedent to government";[95] the system of government was established first, the constitution came later. The communist constitution is not a blueprint for a government to be, but a map of a government that is. For Paine, "government has no right to make itself a party"[96] to the making of constitution; the communist constitutions were effectively granted by the government to the people, although later formally approved by them. Although, realistically, a constitution is never prepared by "the people" but by some more or less responsible "elite," the draftsmen of the communist constitution have not pretended that their constitution responds to the ideas or the will of the people, or that the people had the choice of rejecting the system of government described in the constitution.

The recent communist constitutions claim the authority of popular sovereignty. Earlier, the Soviet constitution had proclaimed the dictatorship of the proletariat, but in 1961, partly in response, no doubt, to prevailing doctrines of the sovereignty of the people (in part, perhaps, in response to national unity and patriotism during the war), the USSR declared that the dictatorship of the proletariat had fulfilled its historic mission and that the Soviet Union was now a state "of the whole people." That has now been expressly declared in the USSR constitution of 1977: "The aims of the dictatorship of the proletariat having been fulfilled, the Soviet state has become a state of the whole people" (Preamble; Article 1). In the preamble, "the Soviet people" "affirm the principles of the social structure and policy of the USSR, and define the rights, freedoms and obligations of citizens, and the principles of the organisation of the socialist state of the whole people, and its aims, and proclaim these in this Constitution." Article 2 provides: "All power in the USSR belongs to the people," and there are other references to the ultimate authority of the people. (The constitution also retains references to "the working people," e.g., Articles 1, 50.) On the other hand, in 1975, doubtless in a desire to reflect on USSR "deviationism," China introduced the dictatorship of the proletariat into its new constitution (Articles 1, 12, 13), even while declaring that power "belongs to the people" (Article 3). These were retained in the 1978 constitution (Articles 1, 3, 19).

The 1977 Soviet constitution provides that the people exercise state power through Soviets of People's Deputies (Article 2). There is a pyramid of workers' representation, which the new Soviet constitution calls "democratic centralism," a hierarchy with "the obligation of lower bodies to observe the decisions of higher ones" (Article 3). "Major matters of state shall be submitted to nationwide discussion and put to a popular vote (referendum)" (Article 5). There is essentially only one party, of limited membership, and strong leadership (and at times, too, there has been a "cult of personality"). The Communist Party is the "leading and guiding force of Soviet society and the nucleus of its political system, of all state organisations and public organisations" (Article 6).

Substantively, both the Soviet and Chinese constitutions, of course, reflect their ideological-socialist character, emphasizing the economic and social concerns of government and the public character of economic enterprise, with minimal private enterprise and property. Prominent has been the duty to work: "The principle applied in the USSR is that of socialism: He who does not work, neither shall he eat." And, "From each according to his ability, to each according to his work" (USSR Constitution, 1936, Article 12; compare PRC, Article 10). In the 1977 USSR constitution, the first provision with its explicit harshness is omitted, but it is presumably still implied the second; since each gets according to his work, presumably he who does not work will not eat. The constitution continues: "Socially useful work and its results determine a person's status in society" (Article 14).

Individual Rights under the Soviet Constitution

Beyond these fundamental socialist principles, the USSR constitution lists the basic rights, freedoms, and duties of citizens, beginning with economic rights: "Citizens of the USSR have the right to work (that is, to guaranteed employment and pay in accordance with the quantity and quality of their work" (Article 40); "the right to rest and leisure," to health protection, to maintenance in old age, in sickness and disability (Articles 41-43); the right to housing and education (Articles 44-45). The 1977 constitution also includes the right to enjoy cultural benefits (Article 46), and "in accordance with the aims of building communism," the freedom of scientific, technical, and artistic work is guaranteed (Article 47); the right to take part in the management and administration of state and public affairs; to submit proposals for improving the activity of public bodies and to criticize their shortcomings (Articles 48-49). In the USSR, women and men have equal rights, and all citizens are equal before the law* (Articles 34-36); discrimination on grounds of race or nationality and advocacy of racial or national exclusiveness, hostility, or contempt are punishable by law (Article 36).

The Soviet constitution also proclaims civil and political rights and freedoms:

> Article 50. In accordance with the interests of the people and in order to strengthen and develop the socialist system, citizens of the USSR are guaranteed freedom of speech, of the press, and of assembly, meetings, street processions and demonstrations.

---

*It is not clear whether equality is modified by whether one does "socially useful work," which "determines a person's status in society" (Article 14).

Exercise of these political freedoms is ensured by putting public buildings, streets and squares at the disposal of the working people and their organisations, by broad dissemination of information, and by the opportunity to use the press, television, and radio.

Article 51. In accordance with the aims of building communism, citizens of the USSR have the right to associate in public organisations that promote their political activity and initiative and satisfaction of their various interests.

Public organisations are guaranteed conditions for successfully performing the functions defined in their rules.

Article 52. Citizens of the USSR are guaranteed freedom of conscience, that is, the right to profess or not to profess any religion, and to conduct religious worship or atheistic propaganda. Incitement of hostility or hatred on religious grounds is prohibited.

In the USSR, the church is separated from the state, and the school from the church.

Article 54. Citizens of the USSR are guaranteed inviolability of the person. No one may be arrested except by a court decision or on the warrant of a procurator.

Article 55. Citizens of the USSR are guaranteed inviolability of the home. No one may, without lawful grounds, enter a home against the will of those residing in it.

Article 56. The privacy of citizens, and of their correspondence, telephone conversations, and telegraphic communications is protected by law.

Article 57. Respect for the individual and protection of the rights and freedoms of citizens are the duty of all state bodies, public organisations, and officials.

Citizens of the USSR have the right to protection by the courts against encroachments on their honour and reputation, life and health, and personal freedom and property.

Article 58. Citizens of the USSR have the right to lodge a complaint against the actions of officials, state bodies and public bodies. Complaints shall be examined according to the procedure and within the time-limit established by law.

Actions by officials that contravene the law or exceed their powers, and infringe the rights of citizens, may be appealed against in a court in the manner prescribed by law.

Citizens of the USSR have the right to compensation for damage resulting from unlawful actions by state organisations and public organisations, or by officials in the performance of their duties.

The articles dealing with the administration of justice include:

Article 155. Judges and people's assessors are independent and subject only to the law.

Article 156. Justice is administered in the USSR on the principle of the equality of citizens before the law and the court.

Article 157. Proceedings in all courts shall be open to the public. Hearings *in camera* are only allowed in cases provided for by law, with observance of all the rules of judicial procedure.

Article 158. A defendant in a criminal action is guaranteed the right to legal assistance.

Article 160. No one may be adjudged guilty of a crime and subjected to punishment as a criminal except by the sentence of a court and in conformity with the law.

Article 161. . . . In cases provided for by legislation citizens shall be given legal assistance free of charge.

The rights and freedoms proclaimed in the USSR constitution are an impressive catalog, matching generally that synthesis of liberty, welfare, and equality that appears in the Universal Declaration of Human Rights and in the international covenants. Some, alas, are missing. There is no counterpart to the provisions in the Universal Declaration (and corresponding provisions in the International Covenant on Civil and Political Rights) against slavery or servitude; torture or cruel, inhuman, or degrading treatment or punishment; arbitrary arrest, detention, or exile; the freedom of movement and residence within one's country and the right to leave one's country and to return.*

Omissions apart, one who thinks of constitutions in Western terms, as implying "constitutionalism," tends to view the Soviet constitution with skepticism, not persuaded that it reflects constitutional government or assures the enjoyment of human rights. Unlike the Constitution of the United States, the Soviet constitution appears to be essentially descriptive, not prescriptive. It does not set forth legal prohibitions ordained by the people upon its government; it is, rather, an ideological statement, a declaration by the government to the world (and perhaps to the people) describing the condition of human rights in the Soviet system and perhaps indicating also the Soviet Union's compliance with the international obligations it has assumed, notably in the International Covenant on Civil and Political Rights. It tells what is, not what should be or must be, what government gives, not what it is required to do or provide. "In the USSR, the law permits individual labour in handicrafts" (Article 17). "The state concerns itself with improving working conditions" (Article 21). "Women and men have equal rights in the USSR" (Article 35). Even the chapter headed "Basic Rights, Freedoms and Duties" seems— judging by official translations into English—to describe the rights citizens have, rather than prescribe what they should or must have. "Citizens of the USSR have the right to rest and

---

*The Soviet constitution also contains no provision corresponding to the presumption of innocence set forth in the Universal Declaration, but the presumption has been considered part of Soviet jurisprudence.[97] There is no equivalent to the writ of habeas corpus in the Soviet system.

The Universal Declaration affirms the parent's prior right to choose the kind of education that shall be given to their children. The Soviet constitution declares that the Soviet system "serves the Communist education and intellectual and physical development of the youth"; it also declares the duty of parents to raise children as worthy members of socialist society (Articles 25, 66). Does the separation of "the school from the church" (Soviet constitution, Article 52) preclude religious schools?

leisure" (Article 41). "Citizens of the USSR are guaranteed freedom of conscience" (Article 52). In some instances, moreover, the constitution provides only that certain rights are protected by law, but does not assert that the protection provided is adequate by human rights standards. "Citizens of the USSR are guaranteed inviolability of the home. No one may, without lawful grounds, enter a home against the will of those residing in it" (Article 55). "The privacy of citizens, and of their correspondence, telephone conversations, and telegraphic communications is protected by law" (Article 56). "Hearings *in camera* are only allowed in cases provided for by law" (Article 157). There is no requirement that the law be consistent with some constitutional or other human rights standard. Article 54 provides that "no one may be arrested except by a court decision or on the warrant of a procurator." There is no requirement that the court decision or the procurator's warrant be consistent with some constitutional or other human rights standard.

This kind of constitution is not to be dismissed or belittled. It may be an ideal for government to aspire to; it may guide government from day to day. A "prescriptive" constitution may not be honored in fact, and a descriptive constitution may accurately reflect an impressive system of rights already in being. Constitutional descriptions or promises, moreover, tend to deter deviations and serve as a basis for domestic protection. That certain rights are defined by law is also not to be dismissed, for the principle of legality is an important right, implying that there must be law and that officials, bureaucrats, and police cannot act by private fiat. (That is a principal element in the requirement of "due process of law" in the United States Constitution.) The procurator general, who is charged with assuring that officials comply with Soviet law (Article 164), can presumably demand compliance with constitutional promises as well (as the Chinese constitution of 1978 expressly provides). Particularly noteworthy is the provision (Article 58) providing for the right of citizens to lodge complaints "against the actions of officials, state bodies and public bodies''; and actions by officials that infringe "rights of citizens, may be appealed against in a court in the manner prescribed by law.'' Some laws implementing this article have been promulgated, and others are apparently in contemplation. If legislation should provide for it, Soviet courts might— in a new departure in Soviet jurisprudence—begin to invalidate acts of lower officials as violating constitutional rights.

For the Western observer, what is missing from the Soviet constitution and the Soviet system is assurance that the constitution will be honored at the highest levels of government. Although the constitution is headed "Fundamental Law" and declares that it shall have "supreme legal force" (Article 173), to the Western observer it seems not to be law at all, surely not higher law. The constitution provides that "all laws and other acts of state bodies shall be promulgated on the basis of and in conformity with it," but what basis is there for confidence that laws will in fact conform to it? (The constitution, moreover, can be amended by the legislature—the Supreme Soviet—by a two-thirds vote [Article 174] and the Supreme Soviet has long been essentially a rubber stamp for its Presidium [Articles 119-23]. There is no judicial review to enforce the constitution against the principal policymakers, or even against others when these do not wish it. The procurator general, who might enforce the constitution against officialdom, cannot enforce it against the Supreme Soviet— to which he is accountable (Article 108). The procurator general himself is also the chief prosecutor, and there is apparently no remedy against his abuse of the criminal process.* When the constitution promises that there will be "legality," that things will be done according to law, there is no assurance against law that is itself oppressive, and no recourse if the law is or becomes inadequate, or is repealed.

---

*Courts provide some safeguards against prosecutorial illegality; whether under Article 58, pp. 62-63 above, the courts might emerge as safeguards against denial of constitutional rights, even by the procurator general, remains to be seen.

The essential characteristics of the USSR constitution, its place in the Soviet political system, and its significance for human rights might best be appreciated by comparing its treatment of freedom of speech and press with that of the U.S. Constitution. The First Amendment to the U.S. Constitution provides that "Congress shall make no law . . . abridging the freedom of speech, or of the press." In the United States, the freedoms of speech and press are thus not promised or granted by the Constitution; they are an inherent, "natural," or contractual right of every individual, antecedent to the Constitution. The Constitution protects them against abridgment by government. (Although the amendment is expressly addressed to the legislature, it has been interpreted to apply to all other parts of government as well.)[98] It is a legal prohibition ordaining government to leave these freedoms alone, and it will be enforced by the courts. Limitations on or exceptions to these rights are not mentioned: there are limitations, we know— conceptual or historical limitations, permitting, for example, abridgment of speech that is libelous or obscene. Overall, too, we have seen, the provision has been interpreted to permit abridgment in the public interest, but only when the public interest is compelling. That judgment is made ultimately by an independent judiciary, one that has in fact frequently nullified governmental abridgments. Except when it is "brigaded to action" or constitutes "incitement" to unlawful action, political speech is virtually free. The Constitution is deemed to reflect the view that freedom to speak or publish, without restraint by government, notably about political matters in criticism of government, is essential to a good society. It assumes that what is important here is freedom from governmental restraint, "political laissez-faire"; it does not require government actively to promote or encourage these freedoms, or to provide access for the individual or for groups to means and channels of communication so as to make communication more effective and the right to communicate more meaningful.[99]

Article 50 of the USSR constitution of 1977* provides:

> In accordance with the interests of the people and in order to strengthen and develop the socialist system, citizens of the USSR are guaranteed freedom of speech, of the press, and of assembly, meetings, street processions and demonstrations.
>
> Exercise of these political freedoms is ensured by putting public buildings, streets and squares at the disposal of the working people and their organisations, by broad dissemination of information, and by the opportunity to use the press, television, and radio.

This article is not a legal prohibition ordained upon the government; it is a declaration of the kinds of freedom there are in the Soviet Union, of their purposes, of how they are used and made effective. It does not prescribe or proclaim any individual right; it describes what the Soviet system does. Freedom of speech or the press is not presumptively unlimited or defined a priori. There is no recourse if the legislature enacts a law that abridges these freedoms or if it fails to assure that they "are guaranteed." What is promised, moreover, is only freedom that is "in accordance with the interests of the people" and that will "strengthen the socialist system"—as government sees it.[100] (The right of association also is promised only "in accordance with the aims of building communism" [Article 51].) The freedoms, moreover, seem principally collective, rather than individual. And the government promotes and encourages their use to strengthen socialism by providing to "the working people and their organisations" the means for effective communication. The freedoms are not designed to permit individuals to oppose or criticize socialism or government policy; the working people have the means of communication so they can participate in government in order to help the

---

*The 1936 text provided that USSR citizens "are guaranteed" these rights "by law." There is no indication that the omission of the words "by law" was designed to effect any change. Among the facilities said to be placed at the disposal of the working people were printing presses and stocks of paper, omitted from the 1977 text.

government achieve socialism.[101] The citizenry is promised effective opportunity to support and participate in government, not freedom from government.

It is not the political freedoms alone—speech, press—that are guaranteed only if exercised in ways consistent with communism; the entire chapter of "Basic Rights, Freedoms and Duties" is subject to the condition that "enjoyment by citizens of their rights and freedoms must not be to the detriment of the interests of society or the state" (Article 39). Article 59, moreover, provides that "citizens' exercise of their rights and freedoms is inseparable from (dependent on?) the performance of their duties and obligations." The USSR constitution declares a catalog of duties*—to observe the constitution, Soviet law, and the standards of socialist conduct and to uphold the honor and dignity of Soviet citizenship (Article 59); to work conscientiously in one's chosen, "socially useful" occupation and "strictly to observe labour discipline" (Article 60); to protect socialist property, safeguard the interests of the Soviet state, defend "the Socialist Motherland" (Articles 61, 62); to perform military service (Article 63); to be uncompromising toward antisocial behavior and to help maintain public order (Article 65); to raise one's children as worthy members of socialist society; to maintain world peace; and so on. Does a citizen risk losing all his rights if he is deficient in any of his duties?

A descriptive constitution, a constitution that is manifesto, not law, a constitution that makes individual rights subject at all times to state interests and to the ideology of communism as these are determined by political authority, need not provide

---

*The U.S. Constitution prescribes no duties, as is perhaps not surprising in a constitution seen as a blueprint of government and a contract imposing limitations on government. See Chapter 1. Even provisions about treason are included only to impose limits on how government may prosecute and punish for it. U.S. Constitution, Article III, Section 3. (In the Soviet constitution, treason is proclaimed "the gravest of crimes against the people" Article 61.) In the United States the legislatures are of course free to impose duties in the public interest but are subject to the Bill of Rights and other constitutional limitations.

for its suspension and need never be suspended. It is sometimes replaced, not to effect change but to describe it, or when a different ideological statement or promise is desired.

The Constitution of the People's Republic of China

The Chinese constitution is the same kind of constitution as that of the USSR—descriptive not prescriptive, manifesto not law; individual rights are subject to political will in the service of communism as perceived by political authorities. There are neither institutions to enforce constitutional declarations of individual rights against all political authority nor other societal forces to render it likely that they will be honored.

The fundamental rights and duties of citizens are briefer and less explicit than in the Soviet constitution. A short-lived 1975 constitution was ideologically purer than the earlier constitution (1954), which was modeled on that of the USSR, and it evinced no strong desire to pay even lip service to constitutionalism and individual rights; the 1978 constitution partly restored the earlier version. The office of the procurator was reinstated (Article 43); the right of the accused to a defense and to a public trial (except in special circumstances) was restored (Article 41). But the earlier constitution's provisions that people's courts administer justice independently and subject only to law was abandoned in 1975; the courts are expressly declared to be responsible and accountable to political authority (Article 42). The earlier provisions that all citizens are equal before the law and that they enjoy freedom of residence and freedom to exchange their residence were deleted in 1975 and have not been restored.[102]

In the Fundamental Rights and Duties of Citizens (Chapter 3), rights now came first:

> Article 44. All citizens who have reached the age of 18 have the right to vote and to stand for election, with the exception of persons deprived of these rights by law.

> Article 45. Citizens enjoy freedom of speech, correspondence,

the press, assembly, association, procession, demonstration and the freedom to strike, and have the right to "speak out freely, air their views fully, hold great debates and write big-character posters."

Article 46. Citizens enjoy freedom to believe in religion and freedom not to believe in religion and to propagate atheism.

Article 47. The citizens' freedom of person and their homes are inviolable.

No citizen may be arrested except by decision of a people's court or with the sanction of a people's procuratorate, and the arrest must be made by a public security organ.

Article 48. Citizens have the right to work. To ensure that citizens enjoy this right, the state provides employment in accordance with the principle of overall consideration, and, on the basis of increased production, the state gradually increases payment for labour, improves working conditions, strengthens labour protection and expands collective welfare.

Article 49. Working people have the right to rest. To ensure that working people enjoy this right, the state prescribes working hours and systems of vacations and gradually expands material facilities for the working people to rest and recuperate.

Article 50. Working people have the right to material assistance in old age, and in case of illness or disability. To ensure that working people enjoy this right, the state gradually expands social insurance, social assistance, public health services, co-operative medical services, and other services.

The state cares for and ensures the livelihood of disabled revolutionary armymen and the families of revolutionary martyrs.

Article 51. Citizens have the right to education. To ensure that citizens enjoy this right, the state gradually increases the number of schools of various types and of other cultural and educational institutions and popularizes education.

The state pays special attention to the healthy development of young people and children.

Article 52. Citizens have the freedom to engage in scientific research, literary and artistic creation and other cultural activities. The state encourages and assists the creative endeavours of citizens engaged in science, education, literature, art, journalism, publishing, public health, sports and other cultural work.

Article 53. Women enjoy equal rights with men in all spheres of political, economic, cultural, social and family life. Men and women enjoy equal pay for equal work.

Men and women shall marry of their own free will. The state protects marriage, the family, and the mother and child.

The state advocates and encourages family planning.

Article 54. The state protects the just rights and interests of overseas Chinese and their relatives.

Article 55. Citizens have the right to lodge complaints with organs of state at any level against any person working in an organ of state, enterprise or institution for transgression of law or neglect of duty. Citizens have the right to appeal to organs of state at any level against any infringement of their rights. No one shall suppress such complaints and appeals or retaliate against persons making them.

Article 56. Citizens must support the leadership of the Communist Party of China, support the socialist system, safeguard the unification of the motherland and the unity of all nationalities in our country and abide by the Constitution and the law.

Article 57. Citizens must take care of and protect public property, observe labour discipline, observe public order, respect social ethics and safeguard state secrets.

Article 58. It is the lofty duty of every citizen to defend the motherland and resist aggression.

It is the honourable obligation of citizens to perform military service and to join the militia according to the law.

Article 59. The People's Republic of China grants the right of residence to any foreign national persecuted for supporting a just cause, for taking part in revolutionary movements or for engaging in scientific work.

Again, this "bill of rights" is essentially descriptive, declaratory. Many fami'iar rights are not mentioned. The rights cited are not expressly limited (as they are in the constitution of the Soviet Union), but "the state safeguards the socialist system, suppresses all treasonable and counter-revolutionary activities, punishes all traitors and counter-revolutionaries, and punishes newborn bourgeois elements and other bad elements" (Article 18). The rights declared are enjoyed only by political grace. The procurator is to ensure observance of the constitution by the bureaucracy, and the citizen may lodge complaints with any organ (Articles 43, 55), but there is no protection against the supreme political authorities or effectively against the failures of the procurator. Both courts and procurator are responsible to the National People's Congress, "the highest organ of state power," and the National People's Congress, which makes laws, can also amend the constitution (Articles 20, 22, 42, 43).

Castro's Cuba

It is instructive to compare the constitution of the state most recently converted to Marxist-Leninist ideology—Castro's Cuba. Unlike the Eastern European socialist countries, which were created and grew up immediately after World War II in the direct and heavy shadow of Soviet power and influence, Cuba became a socialist state in a different geographic and political context, had different traditions, was subject to different influences, and was perhaps more free to be "deviationist," "revisionist," eclectic, as well as idiosyncratic.

Like the Soviet Union, and unlike the People's Republic of China, Cuba has an extensive and detailed constitution. The 1975 Cuban constitution was adopted by "We, the citizens of Cuba," by means of "our free vote in a referendum." In doing so, the preamble asserts, the Cuban people based themselves "on proletarian internationalism" and were guided by "the victorious doctrine of Marxism-Leninism," aware "that only under socialism and communism . . . can the full dignity of the human being be attained." Article 1 of the constitution declares that the "Republic of Cuba is a socialist state of workers and peasants and all other manual and intellectual workers." "In the Republic of Cuba all the power belongs to the working people, who exercise it either directly or through the assemblies of People's Power and other organs of the state which derive their authority from these assemblies" (Article 4). Article 8 provides that the socialist state, inter alia, "guarantees the liberty and the full dignity of man, the enjoyment of his rights, the exercise and fulfillment of his duties and the integral development of his personality." The Cuban constitution has the socialist emphasis on socialist property but recognizes private property in land for small farmers, in a legal residence, in earned savings and personal property (Articles 20-25). "All citizens have equal rights and are subject to equal duties" (Article 40). "Work in a socialist society is a right and duty" (Article 44). The constitution promises a panoply of welfare rights and benefits. It declares in considerable detail the traditional political and civil freedoms, including freedom of speech, press, and assembly; freedom of conscience; inviolability of "personal integrity" in case of arrest; and trial and sentence "with the formalities and guarantees that the law establishes" (Articles 52-60).

The Cuban constitution, then, provides a form of government more communist than Western-democratic. It promises, however, far more than do the Soviet and Chinese constitutions both in civil-political and economic-social rights, and it sounds like a constitution of limitations, not merely of aspirations. It promises the rule of law. But the constitution is not a higher law that effectively limits executive and legislative actions of government. The vindication of constitutional promises is left to political organs, not to an independent judiciary. The citizens have freedom of speech and of the press, but only "in keeping with the objectives of socialist society," and "the law regulates the exercise of these freedoms" (Article 52). "It is illegal and punishable by law to oppose one's faith or religious belief to the Revolution" (Article 54). And "none of the freedoms which are recognized for citizens can be exercised contrary to what is established in the Constitution and the law, or contrary to the existence and objectives of the socialist state, or contrary to the decision of the Cuban people to build socialism and communism" (Article 61).

In sum, to the Western observer, the communist constitutions, even on their face, describe neither bona fide popular sovereignty or representative government nor meaningful limitations on high levels of government. They reflect inadequate regard for the political and civil rights of the individual as against the group. They promise no freedom of movement and other autonomies. In particular, they permit little political freedom and are prone to gross political repression. In China and the USSR, the constitutions do not promise authentic due process of criminal law, that is, they do not promise apolitical prosecution, trial, and punishment, freedom from undue inquisition and detention, from torture and cruel and unusual treatment or punishment. Effectively, they offer freedom of speech, press, and assembly only to support socialism as determined by authority. And unlike Western countries that have no effective legal constitution binding all government (e.g., Great Britain), what we know about conditions in these countries does not allow us to assume that in these regards human rights, especially political rights, fare far better in fact than the constitutions promise. Granting that all radical revolutions are violent and "purgative" at their inception, uprooting the old order to build a new society for the future;* granting that the admitted terrors of the Stalin regime

---

*In contrast, Lord Acton said of the American Revolution that "no other revolution was ever conducted with so much moderation." (But he also considered that no other revolution "ever proceeded from so slight a cause."[103] The U.S. Constitution was even further away from revolutionary ideology. See Chapter 1 above.

or even of the Cultural Revolution and other postrevolution disturbances in China were fortuitous,[104] not inherent in Marxist-Leninist socialism—all the regimes that have existed in both communist China and the Soviet Union, and in Castro's Cuba, have reflected the dangers for human rights in unrepresentative, monarchic (or oligarchic) unaccountable government. Power is in the hands of too few, and it is political, not legal, power. (Critics insist that workers' representation does not make government responsible to them but is used as the vehicle for making workers responsive to government.) Dissent and dissidence are often crimes and sometimes approach treason; investigation and detention have no effective limits or safeguards.[105] Human rights, we know, can flourish without a "higher-law constitution," without judicial review, if there are other historical, cultural, or societal forces to support them. The communist societies, however, are still closed, and the condition of human rights is largely immune to internal criticism and not sufficiently sensitive to external influences. In the USSR, there are no traditions and few institutions supporting individual human rights. Against state policy that flouts individual rights there are no officials, no courts, no press, no nongovernmental organizations. Some academics and writers protest violations of human rights, but, significantly, they and we, and the Soviet government, all call them "dissidents." In China, the traditions supporting human rights were attacked by the revolution. There are new institutions, but their focus, apparently, is on duties to the group, not on the rights of the individual.

The Soviet and the Chinese (and Cuban) authorities, and others, would no doubt insist that the people of the Soviet Union and China (and Cuba) are content. They can point to important advances in the economic and social welfare of the masses of the people and to the elimination of gross inequalities. They may say that they are achieving something more important than individualistic, bourgeois, and outdated "rights." China in particular can claim that it presents a model that is far more relevant and more attractive, especially to developing states, than the Western libertarian heritage.

Doubtless, the overwhelming majority of people in the Soviet Union and China (and Cuba) are not "dissident." The vast majority of them live better than their ancestors. Surely, no friend of human rights ought to underestimate a society's commitment that no one shall starve or remain illiterate or even be out of work. He ought not assume that political-civil rights cannot prosper under socialism and that they have no future in these two great countries or in Cuba. He might nonetheless ask whether the earlier communist promise stressing rights ("to each according to his need") is not more conducive to individual welfare than the present stress on duties ("to each according to his work"). He is entitled, I think, to ask whether the communist commitment really requires the total political, economic, and social regimentation that these countries still impose. And if indeed that commitment requires the subordination of the individual, the sacrifice of some for the benefit of all, of the present for the future (even if that future were admittedly worthy and sure to be realized),* he may perhaps ask whether it is worth the human cost.

In human rights, as in other respects, there has been a measure of "convergence" between the Western libertarian democracies and the communist "people's democracies." The West, we saw, has moved to provide basic human needs to all and to put some limit on economic inequalities; communism,

---

*Edmund Burke referred to society as "a partnership not only of those who are living, but between those who are living, those who are dead, and those who are to be born."[106] But the terms of partnership differ widely in different societies and in different times and circumstances. Western societies might be charged with paying too much attention to the dead (to their ancestral constitutions and other values) and too little to the unborn, resisting long-term planning, being improvident with environment and resources, and showing little concern for what they bequeath to the future. Socialist states are committed to planning and presumably include in their plans the unborn, at least the near generations. But even apart from the costs of revolution, in which many living were sacrificed to the future, in the principal socialist states the rights of all the living are sharply limited for the sake of a hoped-for better society for the unborn.

we see, has been moved to make at least some commitment to civil rights and political freedoms. Is it beyond hope that the next generation of communist constitutions, or the one after, might be substantially better in principle and more meaningful in fact?

Constitutions and Human Rights in the Third World

Unlike the First World (the West) and the Second (the communist bloc), the "Third World" is not, at bottom, an ideological category. If it has any common ideology, it is "development," nation building, and modernization. Many of its member states describe themselves as socialist, but most are not essentially Marxist and follow no other identifiable socialist ideology. They are socialist in stressing economic and social development, in nationalizing important segments of the economy, and in subordinating individual to group interests. Although the institutions and policies by which governments pursue development may deeply implicate human rights, other forces and factors explain the variety in political and social institutions and in the condition of human rights in different Third World states.

The Third World includes states in every continent: some are very old (e.g., Egypt), some modern but established (as in Latin America), and many newly born; a few are rich, some very poor. Almost all Third World states have constitutions including bills of rights, most of which were drafted after World War II on the model of the U.S. Bill of Rights, the French Declaration, the Universal Declaration of Human Rights, or the European Convention on Human Rights. These bills of rights are not grossly different, though the same words do not always mean the same things, and many constitutions have special features reflecting local history and other local circumstances.

Some differences are due to the age and birth date of the constitution and of the society. Constitutions for older societies are likely to reflect an established society, with a legal system, traditions, and societal assumptions that are taken for granted and do not have to be affirmed in the constitution. Constitutions for new or radically transformed societies might feel compelled to articulate an ideology or other selected values, as in the 1975 constitution of Cuba. The circumstances in which a constitution was drafted will help decide what is deemed "constitution-worthy," deserving enshrinement or status as higher law difficult to modify. (Compare the provisions in the U.S. Bill of Rights on the right to bear arms or quarter troops [Amendments 2, 3], a product of those times, which would doubtless not be in a U.S. bill of rights promulgated today.)

There are local differences among constitutions in almost every respect, many of which have implications for human rights.[107] The right to vote is universal in many states, but in an earlier Cuban constitution (1940) the military and the police were denied the vote (Article 99d); army privates apparently do not vote in Brazil. (Compare article 147[2] of the 1967 constitution, amended 1969.) Some states have compulsory voting, at least for literate citizens—e.g., Brazil (1969, Article 147); Guatemala (1965, Article 19). Where government is representative, there are local variations: India provided special representation for the underprivileged and untouchables (1949, as modified through 1972, Articles 330, 334); Cyprus provided proportional representation for the Greek and Turkish communities with a built-in veto (1960, Articles 62, 78)—until the arrangement fell apart in 1974. Pakistan set aside a number of seats for women for a number of years (1973, Article 51[4]). Many constitutions provide for only one party, e.g., Tanzania (1965, Article 3); some permit several parties but outlaw one or more (e.g., "Parties which . . . seek to impair or abolish the free democratic basic order or to endanger the existence of the . . . Federal Republic of Germany," Article 21[2], 1949 amended through 1973; and the Communist party explicitly in several Latin American countries, e.g., Guatemala, Article 27.)

Most constitutions promise freedom of opinion, speech, press, but there is often punishment for "abuse" (Brazil, Article 153[8]) and provision for derogation or suspension in "emergency" (Egypt 1971, Article 48). Some provide such freedoms so long as they are not "hostile to the Socialist System" (Romania, 1952, Article 29) or "they do not attack fundamental principles of the State" (Spain, 1945, amended 1967, Article 12), or so long as they remain "within the limits of public interest and the principles of the revolution" (Libya, 1969, Article 13). Some prohibit propaganda for war (Venezuela, 1961, Article 66) or interference with international relations (India, Article 19[2]) or ethnic propaganda (Ivory Coast, 1960, Article 6); some "except heretical books and materials hurtful to the perspicuous religion (of Islam)" (Iran, Article 20, Supplementary Constitutional Law of October 8, 1907). Some forbid ownership of press and radio by foreigners (Brazil, Article 174) or prohibit the press from receiving foreign funds without approval (Paraguay, 1967, Article 74).

Constitutions generally provide for freedom of religion, but Malaysia controls propagation of other religions among Muslims (1957, Article 11[4]). Some forbid various religious practices (by statute, in the name of "Africanization," Zaire forbids saints' names).

The establishment of religion exists in various forms. "The Sabbath Day shall be sacred in Tonga for ever and it shall not be lawful to do work or play games or trade on the Sabbath. And any agreement made or document witnessed on this day shall be counted void and shall not be recognized by the Government" (1967, Article 6). Some require the individual to contribute to his/her church (Denmark, 1953, Article 68), but in Iceland one may contribute instead to the university (1944, Article 64).

Constitutions generally proclaim freedom from slavery and forced labor, but some permit forced labor for reasons or purposes specified by law (El Salvador, 1962, Article 155). Professional services of a social character are compulsory in

Mexico (1917 amended through 1973, Article 5), and compulsory military service is accepted virtually everywhere. The Federal Republic of Germany provides for conscientious objection as a matter of constitutional right (Article 12a). Equality is now commonly proclaimed, but in Liberia only blacks can be citizens (1847, modified through 1955, Article 5, sec. 13); in Egypt the state guarantees to every woman "coordination between the woman's duties to the family and her career in society, and equality with man in the fields of political, social, cultural and economic life" but stresses that this will be accomplished "without any violation of the rules of Islamic Sharia" (Article 11).

Criminal procedure widely promises the rights with which we are familiar. Some states outlaw trials in absentia (Uruguay, 1967, Article 21). Some provide the right "to a defense" (cf. the 1936 Soviet constitution, Article 111); some also specify the right to counsel (Egypt, Article 67). Capital punishment is outlawed in many states; some preclude capital punishment for women or for persons over a given age (Guatemala, Article 54). In some states, there is also a maximum prison sentence (Venezuela, Article 60[7]). Search and seizure is barred in some states during night hours (Guatemala, Article 57). Some extend a privilege not to testify against blood relatives (Bolivia, 1967, Article 14).

Economic and social rights are variously worded. In Uruguay every person has a right to a decent home (Article 45); in Paraguay to a home standing on its own land (1967, Article 83). In a number of constitutions, the state is obligated to provide work and welfare (Denmark, Article 75); some add "in so far as economic development and its financial resources permit" (Turkey, 1961, Article 53). Some socialist constitutions severely restrict private enterprise; some encourage it (Malta, 1964, Article 19). Some combat intemperance (India, Article 47). Most provide a right to universal education (Cuba, 1975, Article 50; Guatemala, Article 94). Italy specifies a right to "institute legal proceedings for the protection of their own rights and legitimate interests" (1947, Article 24, cf. Article 57 of the 1977 USSR constitution). Mexico promises free access to the courts (Article 17). Ecuador provides that the state must protect a child from the moment of conception (1967, Article 30).

Particular variations apart, the proliferation of constitutions and bills of rights doubtless responds to widespread and prevailing conceptions—at least slogans—of "constitutionalism," "democracy," "popular sovereignty" however defined (or undefined), and to a *zeitgeist* of aspiration and an ideal of progress. The constitutions originally provided both domestic and international legitimacy and in many instances were a condition of decolonization or statehood. But especially as the ideology of development becomes stronger, constitutions have been condemned by some as unrealistic and inappropriate Western impositions, undesirable and dangerous even, because they put brakes on governments that, they say, are rather in need of accelerators. Some states, in fact, soon shed their constitutions or modified them to more "efficient" models. But most constitutions have survived, and their continued significance for human rights should not be underestimated: they represent values and hopes; they reflect, and contribute to, a measure of enjoyment of rights at least "in principle," "normally"; and they have educational and some deterrent influence in almost every country. Even when a constitution is suspended, the fact that military and other extraconstitutional rulers feel obliged to suspend the constitution speaks to its deterrent influence. Suspension, moreover, is recognized as an extraordinary condition, and while it lasts, it is a constant reminder to its abnormal character. But as maps to the condition of human rights in particular countries at a particular time, they differ widely in accuracy; many of them require serious qualification.

Some Third World states see and style themselves "revolutionary." Although many states or governments grew out of revolution (as indeed did the United States, the Soviet Union, and the People's Republic of China), not every revolution or *soi-disant* revolutionary government creates a revolutionary society, and not all revolutionary societies long remain so. But there are particular implications for human rights in all revolutionary times, and some revolutionary regimes are and long remain committed to an ideology of "revolution," of reordering society radically and quickly. In different ways and for varying lengths of time, revolution has been a dominant theme in China and Cuba, Cambodia and Vietnam, Ghana, Guinea, and Tanzania, Algeria, Chile, and others.

Revolutions are in a hurry, at least at the beginning. Some are building new states, modernizing a society and developing an economy. They are more concerned with economic and social planning for the future than with present rights. Being in a hurry, the revolution has no patience for obstacles, and individual rights, especially so-called political and civil rights, seem to be an obstacle. In only few cases, for example, Tanzania under Julius Nyerere, is attention given to individual rights and an effort made to build institutions and policies that might protect them even in a revolutionary context and in a single-party socialist state.[108]

Revolutionary societies apart (and revolutionary societies do not usually remain so very long), Third World states run the whole spectrum from libertarian democracy to authoritarian barbarism. Most of them fall in between, and the condition of human rights varies and is variable. The student of constitutions will note that in too many cases constitutions are inadequate to provide "constitutionalism." Many a constitution is only hortatory, a "manifesto," "a splendid bauble,"[109] not higher law, and governments are not always and in all circumstances sensitive to constitutional declarations and promises. Some constitutions are subject to general principles of interpretation or derogation, permitting governmental authorities to limit rights as required by "national unity and integrity, national security, national economy, public safety, public order, [and the] protection of public health or morals";[110] or to respect rights only in conformity with the "interests of the socialist community" or with the "revolutionary national and progressive trend."[111] Although derogations from various rights as required by "national security" are permitted everywhere, in some states the claims of national security reach ludicrous lengths and readily swallow important rights.

Although there is virtually universal obeisance—at least lip service—to democracy, too often the sovereignty of the people is satisfied by occasional plebiscites, not by authentic, accountable, representative government and free political institutions, on which other political-civil rights ultimately depend. Often there is essentially one-party, often one-man government; there is little meaningful political opposition, and opposition is often viewed as crime, akin to treason. In many states there are few effective limitations on government. Rights are not higher law, and, of course, there is no independent judiciary to enforce them against government. Even where there is judicial review in principle, there may be little in fact if the judiciary is neither independent nor bold (and even effective judicial review can afford no greater protection than does the constitution it enforces). Often missing also are traditions of individual worth and respect for rights, an independent and alert press free from censorship, and an aware, activist elite concerned for human rights. There are deep prejudices; minorities often suffer invidious discriminations, deportations, sometimes massacres. There have been authoritative reports of massive tribal massacres in Burundi, of the elimination of masses of "communists" in Indonesia, of many millions in Cambodia. There are many reports of less repressive societies.[112]

Perhaps the most serious qualification of the condition of human rights is the provision in almost every constitution for suspension or derogation of rights in time of emergency. Thus, Article 22 of the Indian constitution, though regulating preventive detention, leaves the door open for laws such as the

Maintenance of Internal Security Act of 1971, which allows the detention of anyone the government "believes . . . is acting in a manner prejudicial to the state." Compare the Republic of South Africa, which under its South African Terrorism Act allows the detention of anyone the police have "reason to believe" is "a terrorist or is withholding from the South African Police any information relating to terrorists."[113] Colombia, hardly the most repressive of states and hardly an exceptional example, has been wholly without emergency rule during only two of the past thirty years.[114] Often an emergency can be declared by executive fiat, and the executive can then rule by decree. Emergency often also brings into play press censorship and individual detention, often unreviewable, often for extended and extendable periods or indefinitely. By reports of the government itself, 50,000 political prisoners were detained in Indonesia, most of them for ten years, most of them without trial.[115] There have been authoritative reports of detention and torture in Brazil and Chile in the middle 1970s. India, long an inspiring example of a new liberal democracy, beginning in 1975 suffered two years of government by decree, mass detention, and the curtailment of liberties; in 1976 its constitution was amended to eliminate any constitutional limitations on parliament and to abolish judicial review for violations of individual rights.[116] Even an independent judiciary cannot protect individual rights against emergency rule where the constitution permits emergency rule. Emergency rule, moreover, tends to end any judicial independence or to neutralize or disarm it: in India, for example, during the repression years the government decreed that the grounds for arrest need not be disclosed, apparently in order to make it impossible for the courts to review their legal adequacy.[117] (Happily, new elections in 1977 have reversed the trend and promised to restore at least some of the lost freedoms.)

*　　*　　*

The condition of human rights in different countries is

difficult to appraise.[118] There is no universally accepted test by which one can determine the health or unhealth of human rights generally, or of many particular rights; there is no universally accepted hierarchy of rights that would permit giving high grades for better performance in regard to some rights if not others. Information, moreover, is difficult to obtain and is often unreliable, and the significance even of accurate data is not self-defining. Different countries act better or worse in regard to different rights. Most governments are apparently trying to improve the economic and social welfare of the masses of their people; in many countries, liberty suffers. Although political-civil rights without concern for welfare is now increasingly rare, apparent concern for economic welfare without respect for political-civil rights and freedom is all too common.

I have described the state of human rights in national societies, at least in conception and principle. No state, I conclude, is perfect in regard to human rights, and only a few are unspeakable. All systems and all societies now recognize some individual rights. Every state has a legal system, reflecting a measure of order, itself an important right and implying others. All societies respect many other rights in "normal," as distinguished from highly "politicized," contexts, for the acquiescent as distinguished from the dissident. In all societies there are difficult issues of accommodation between individual rights and public good, or between competing individual rights. All systems have limitations on rights for overriding values, all permit deviations from normal human rights in abnormal situations, for example, in war.

The principal differences among systems and countries, then, may appear as differences of degree. But those differences are critical. By Western standards, the countries that substantially respect the rights of man today are not many. After World War II, the Western democracies hoped to show their way to the world, and indeed they wrote it into the Universal Declaration of Human Rights[119] and into the constitutions of states. Since then, a hundred new states have come to life, and almost every one began with a constitution, popular sovereignty, universal suffrage, and a bill of rights. But many of these states and some older ones have given way to autarchy or oligarchy, civilian or military, to government by decree. Liberty without representative government is not impossible. Even military governments have not necessarily been more repressive than civilian governments, even than elected civilian governments, and some military governments have provided relief from civilian oppression, corruption, and disorder—relief that is itself a human right. But military governments are not representative and do not satisfy a human right to self-government, are not accountable, cannot be counted on to remain unoppressive, and usually do not respect other political-civil rights and freedoms or provide institutions to safeguard them. Many states now have a dependent judiciary, politicized justice, a controlled press.[120] There are gaps, or worse, between aspiration or protestation or even law, and reality. Some societies make some violations of rights national policy—e.g., apartheid in the Republic of South Africa—and such violations are more difficult to eradicate, of course, than those due merely to the inefficiency, negligence, indifference, or even commitments of particular regimes or officials. The common urge for rapid economic development and the common struggle with economic depression tempt governments to cut corners with rights, to copy the more regimented societies in sacrificing individual liberty and autonomy. Liberty promised is not enjoyed by those who dare to assert it. Equality proclaimed, and even written into law, does not assure it to tribal or other minorities. Internal resistance to violations of human rights is exceptional (and often dangerous), and external scrutiny is limited and of limited effect.[121] And the loss of political rights and the abortion of promised civil rights have not yet led to wide and substantial enjoyment of economic-social rights.

Whether a society has more or less respect for human rights

will be reflected to some substantial extent in its constitution and bill of rights. But what is in the constitution and how much it is realized will depend on societal conditions and attitudes—on whether a society has achieved more, or less, freedom from want; on the promise of political, economic, and social development and stability; on representative and accountable government, itself a basic right and one on which all other rights may depend; on maintaining apolitical justice and an independent judiciary; on a strong, bold, independent press, free from censorship; on other official and unofficial institutions; on popular awareness and concern; on external intellectual and political influences, including the concern, scrutiny, protest, and pressure of international organizations and other governments generally (as on South Africa) or of particular governments, e.g., the government of the United States in the late 1970s.[122] It will depend, too, on a society's commitments, traditions, values, and attitudes. Does a society emphasize the individual or the group? Does it stress individual rights or duties? Does it value rights more than it fears their abuse? Does it see obligations to the individual and, if so, according to his need? his work? his worth? his merit? his loyalty?[123] Does it stress strong activist government or limitations on government, freedom or economic welfare? Does it tend to sacrifice the present to the future or the future to the present, and what is its particular accommodation of their respective claims?

In a world of nation-states, the relation of an individual to his society is the concern of each society and its government. When a society fails, when national constitutions, laws, institutions, and societal forces remain inadequate to sustain commitment to human rights, hope for individual rights come to depend on forces beyond and above the nation-state.

THREE

HUMAN RIGHTS ABOVE AND
BEYOND NATIONS

That "natural rights" are nowhere realized automatically;
that national constitutions and bills of rights are not
everywhere effective law; that national societies have not done
as well as they might by human rights, and that periodically
some of them have behaved horrendously, culminating in the
unspeakable horrors of nazism—all these have inspired efforts
to protect and promote human rights above and beyond
national frontiers. In our time, human rights have become a
principal activity of international governmental and nongovernmental organizations and have led to an international
law imposing human rights obligations on states. Human
rights have figured prominently in relations between nations
and have been grist for other transnational mills.

The International Human Rights Movement

Concern by some governments and their citizens with the
condition of individuals in other countries is not new.
Centuries ago, princes and popes interceded for coreligionists
and others in various countries. The nineteenth century saw a
number of "humanitarian interventions" by big powers,
diplomatically and even militarily, to protest, or end, or
prevent massacres, pogroms, and other atrocities. These,
however, were personal expressions of "noblesse oblige" or

extraordinary reactions to egregious events; they were sharp deviations from the international political system's assumptions that how a state treated its own citizens was its own business. Surely there was generally no serious disposition to render the individual human being in his own country a subject of international diplomacy and law, nor to establish international institutions to promote individual rights and international law to govern a state's behavior in regard to such internal affairs.

Human rights were generally not the stuff of international politics or law until after World War II, but individual welfare was not wholly beyond the ken of the international system even before then. In idea, international law and human rights were linked even before the eighteenth-century heyday of rights theory, both having natural law antecedents and common progenitors in Grotius, Vattel, and Locke.[1] In fact, too, international law early included some human rights obligations in treaties undertaking tolerance for heterodox religious worship and freedom from civil disabilities for religious dissenters. Customary international law has also long imposed on states a responsibility not to deny justice to aliens.

Obligations to respect religious dissenters and aliens had humanitarian consequences, of course, but their inspiration was political. Christian princes had gone to war on behalf of coreligionists in other countries, and religious tolerance was a condition of peace in war-weary Europe; agreements for mutual tolerance made possible the establishment of the secular state and the rise of modern international law. Powerful states exporting people, goods, and capital to other countries in the age of mercantilism insisted on law that would protect the interests these represented: "denial of justice" to an alien was an offense to the state whose nationality he bore[2] and jeopardized the state's economic and political interests. (Aliens who were "stateless," who had no nationality, therefore had no remedy for denial of justice, since no state was offended by such denials.) States insisted on an international standard of justice (rooted in natural law) for their nationals abroad even if these states themselves might not necessarily recognize this standard for their citizens at home. In the last century, in substantial part to protect their own nationals, nations sought to mitigate the horrors of war by developing law to forbid particularly cruel weapons, and to protect prisoners of war and civilian populations during war.

I stress the political inspirations for the older international law of human rights, but I do not imply that it was without humanitarian concern. It is significant that centuries ago, rulers and governments were offended, sometimes to the point of war, by violations of the "human rights" of individuals; that rulers and other less-than-democratic governments cared to make war less terrible for their individual citizens, perhaps even at some possible cost to their military interests. Humanitarian concerns also motivated the "humanitarian interventions" in the nineteenth century, although they could hardly claim that the mistreatment of local inhabitants violated any international norm or obligation.

We come closer to the mood of modern law in our century. Following World War I, in order to remove a potential cause of international friction or war, several states were asked to assume obligations, in minority treaties guaranteed by the League of Nations, to respect the rights of ethnic, national, linguistic, religious, or other minorities among their inhabitants.[3] The League of Nations Covenant provided that the mandate system established for dependent areas should be governed by the principle that "the well being and development of such peoples form a sacred trust of civilization," and imposed "conditions which will guarantee freedom of conscience and religion" and other rights. Members of the League undertook "to secure just treatment of the native inhabitants of territories under their control." The mandatory power was required to promote the welfare and rights of the inhabitants.[4] The years following World War I also saw a major development in the law of human rights, a development

that is often overlooked and commonly underestimated: the
International Labor Office (now the International Labor
Organization [ILO]) launched a series of conventions setting
minimum standards for labor and a variety of other social
conditions. (These are highly impressive and still important
even in the day of newer law: more than 100 of these
conventions have come into force, and many of them have been
accepted by many states.)[5]

One may plausibly question whether those developments,
too, reflected an authentic, altruistic concern for human rights.
Minority treaties were imposed on nations defeated in the war,
on newly created states, and on a few others; they were not
universal norms required of the big and the powerful as well.
The mandate provisions were essentially hortatory, a small
rhetorical price for continuing "imperialism" instead of
granting the territories self-determination and self-government. Even the ILO conventions, perhaps, served less-than-
altruistic purposes. Improvement in the conditions of labor
was perhaps capitalism's defense against the specter of
spreading socialism, which had already established itself in the
largest country in Europe. States, moreover, have direct interests in the conditions of labor in countries with which they
compete in a common market; surely, states impelled to
improve conditions at home would be reluctant to do so unless
others did the same, lest the increase in their costs of production
render their products noncompetitive.

Broader, patently idealistic law came in the wake of Hitler.
The international human rights movement was born in, and
out of, World War II. The proclaimed aims of that war were not
merely "to make the world safe for democracy" (as in World
War I) but to establish individual rights—the Four Freedoms—
for everyone in every country. And that slogan, which served to
rally the war effort, also inspired the planning for the postwar
world. When the war ended, the victors imposed human rights
obligations in peace treaties and included human rights
violations in the Nuremberg Charter and prosecutions;

occupying powers presided at the incorporation of human rights safeguards into new constitutions and laws for West Germany, Japan, and Austria. But these were not universal, or even reciprocal, undertakings applicable to the victors as well.

It was the UN Charter that ushered in the new international concern with human rights everywhere. It replaced the League of Nations's concentration on the rights of minorities in selected countries with heed to the rights of all individuals everywhere.[6] (The new commitment to "self-determination," together with universal human rights, it was apparently thought, would eliminate the minorities problem: some minorities would become independent by self-determination; the rest would find their rights protected equally with majorities by universal commitment to human rights for all.) The preamble of the UN Charter reaffirms "faith in fundamental human rights, in the dignity and worth of the human person, in the equal rights of men and women," and declares the determination of peoples "to promote social progress and better standards of life in larger freedom." The purposes of the UN include international cooperation "in promoting and encouraging respect for human rights and for fundamental freedoms for all without distinction as to race, sex, language, or religion" (Article 1, 55[c]). Human rights are among the responsibilities for study and recommendation of the General Assembly (Article 13) and the Economic and Social Council (Article 62[2]), and a commission on human rights is expressly required (Article 68). Human rights provisions are prominent in Chapters XI and XII dealing with non-self-governing territories and international trusteeship. Members pledged themselves to cooperate with the UN organization for the achievement of its human rights purposes (Article 56).

The various UN bodies have devoted years and arduous effort to promoting human rights. Human rights have been on every agenda of every body and have become a staple of UN activity. A universal declaration of human rights was prepared and adopted. Even particular human rights violations have received attention, early as in the case of Russian wives of non-Russians and in the treatment of Indians in South Africa, more recently in other cases. Some violations—e.g., apartheid in South Africa—are perennially on the UN agenda. Other violations in other places—the treatment of Soviet Jews, allegations of torture by Chile—were the subject of extended international debate over many years. Despite resistance, it was established that UN preoccupation with human rights was not intervention in matters that are essentially within the domestic jurisdiction of a state, in part because UN consideration was not intervention, even more because human rights were not a domestic, but an international, concern.

The UN Charter also ushered in new international law of human rights. The new law buried the old dogma that the individual is not a "subject" of international politics and law and that a government's behavior toward its own nationals is a matter of domestic, not international, concern. It penetrated national frontiers and the veil of sovereignty. It removed the exclusive identification of an individual with his government. It gave the individual a part in international politics and rights in international law, independently of his government. It also gave the individual protectors other than his government, indeed protectors and remedies against his government.

The international law of human rights differs from other international law in its motivations and impulses as well. Generally, international law is made, international obligations are undertaken, to serve common or reciprocal national interests,[7] and early human rights laws, too, we have seen, largely served states' own political or economic purposes. The move to a comprehensive human rights law also sought to appeal to national and transnational interests, perhaps in an effort to de-emphasize its radical nature. Human rights, it was urged, were related to international peace, for states that violate human rights at home are not trustworthy in international relations, and violations of those rights afford occasions, temptations, and pretexts for interventions or war. (The latter argument has since found instances to support it, e.g., as regards racism in southern Africa.) The international human rights law had a different kind of political motivation: namely, states that had had minority treaties or human rights provisions in peace treaties imposed on them resented being singled out and sought to universalize their undertakings. But whatever reasons (or rationalizations) were provided to mask it, the fact is that the new comprehensive international human rights law generally serves no patent, particular national interest. It is essentially ideological, idealistic, humanitarian; its true and deep purpose is to improve the lot of individual men and women everywhere, particularly where national institutions and nonlegal international forces are not adequate—a unique and revolutionary purpose for international law.

The international law of human rights parallels and supplements national law, superseding and supplying the deficiencies of national constitutions and laws, but it does not replace and indeed depends on national institutions. The constituency in every society that supports human rights law is different from the constituency that supports, say, international trade agreements, or military alliances, or peaceful settlements, or even international organization and cooperation. The pressures on a government to adhere to international human rights law are also different from those to adhere to other law, and, indeed, a state's adherence to human rights conventions is far less important if in fact it behaves at home, toward its own, consistently with their terms.

Like other international law, human rights law is made by treaty or convention; there is also customary human rights law made by national practice with a developing sense of legal obligation. The declarations and resolutions of UN organs and other international bodies on human rights may have greater weight in achieving international law here than on other matters, since they purport to express the conscience of mankind on a matter of conscience. And though all law making is a political process, humanitarianism, we shall see, has its own politics, in both making and enforcing law.

In themselves, the normative human rights provisions of the UN Charter are general and preliminary: essentially, by Articles 55 and 56 member states pledge themselves to take joint and separate action in cooperation with the United Nations to achieve respect for human rights.[8] Human rights are not defined or specified in the charter, and there is no clear undertaking not to commit one or another violation. The institutions, procedures, and programs for inducing national respect for rights, for monitoring the condition of human rights in different countries, and for preventing, deterring, or ending violations are not provided. (Had these been attempted at the time, many think, they would not have been acceptable, even in the mood of idealism and cooperation that immediately followed World War II.)

The UN Charter was followed by the Universal Declaration of Human Rights,[9] a remarkable juncture of political-civil and economic-social rights, with equality and freedom from discrimination a principal and recurrent theme. It declared the rights to life, liberty, and security of person, to fair criminal process, to freedom of conscience, thought, expression, association, and privacy; the right to seek and enjoy asylum, to leave one's country and return to it, rights to marriage and family, and rights of property. It declared the will of the people to be the basis of the authority of government, and provided for universal suffrage and bona fide elections. It speaks of the right to work and leisure, health care, and education. (Because the Declaration was designed to be universal, it included provisions that some national constitutions assumed and took for granted or did not consider necessary or "constitution-worthy," for example, the fundamentality of the family [Article 16(3)] or the right of political asylum.)[10]

The Universal Declaration was not generally conceived as law but as "a common standard of achievement" for all to aspire to;* hence its approval without dissent. The communist countries (Belorussian SSR, Czechoslovakia, Poland, Ukrainian SSR, USSR, and Yugoslavia), the Union of South Africa, and Saudi Arabia abstained. Some thought that the United Nations should rest on the Declaration and concentrate on encouraging states to raise their national norms and conform their national behavior to its standards. Instead, governments moved to convert the Declaration into binding legal norms. The process was very, very long. In some part, this was due to the ever-increasing number of states, all of which joined in the process and, of course, slowed the negotiations. In part, delay was due to the differences between a declaration and a binding covenant. Some states that had been prepared to declare a general principle wished it carefully defined and circumscribed if it were to be clearly a legal obligation with legal consequences, for though no state was compelled to adhere to any draft covenant that might emerge, most states wanted something they might be able to adopt if it became desirable; they were reluctant, moreover, to have a covenant adopted as the international norm—in whose light their behavior would appear to be wanting. The process was also extended, on the other hand, because there were strong pressures to develop and elaborate the generalities of the Declaration and give them more specific content so that they would afford greater protection. The Declaration, moreover, did not provide for its implementation, but many sessions were spent debating and elaborating means to enforce the new, emerging legal undertakings.

In substantial part, it took eighteen years to convert the

---

*Even at the time, however, a few saw the Declaration as interpreting and particularizing the general provisions of the charter and therefore partaking of its binding legal character.[11] Later, General Assembly resolutions unanimously proclaimed the duty of states to "fully and faithfully observe" the provisions of the Declaration;[12] unofficial international assemblies and conferences at Montreal and Tehran in 1968 resolved to similar effect. At the Conference on Security and Cooperation in Europe (Helsinki 1975), respect for the Declaration was included among the principles guiding relations between participating states.[13] In time, indeed, others began to speak of the Declaration as though it had the effect of law.

Declaration into convention because it was necessary to accommodate, bridge, submerge, and conceal deep divisions and differences, especially between democratic-libertarian and socialist-revolutionary states—differences in fundamental conceptions about the relation of society to the individual, about the purposes of government, about the individual's rights and duties, about priorities and preferences among them. The original drafts included only political and civil rights, but economic and social rights were added early. Western states then fought for, and obtained, a division into two covenants, a Covenant on Civil and Political Rights, another Covenant on Economic, Social and Cultural Rights. They insisted that economic and social rights were essentially aspirations or plans, not rights, since their realization depended on economic resources and on controversial economic theory and ideology. These, they said, were not appropriate subjects for binding obligations and should not be allowed to dilute the legal character of provisions honoring political-civil rights; states prepared to assume obligations to respect political-civil rights should not be discouraged from doing so by requiring of them impossible social-economic commitments.[14]

The two covenants recognize the difference in the character of rights in various subtle ways. For example, the Covenant on Civil and Political Rights is drafted in terms of the individual's rights: e.g., "Every human being has the inherent right to life." "No one shall be held in slavery." "All persons shall be equal before the courts and tribunals." The Covenant on Economic, Social and Cultural Rights, on the other hand, speaks only to the states, not to the individual: "The States Parties to the present Covenant recognize the right to work." "The States Parties . . . undertake to ensure . . . the right of everyone to form trade unions." "The States Parties . . . recognize the right of everyone to education." There was wide agreement and clear recognition that the means required to enforce or induce compliance with social-economic undertakings were different from the means required for civil-political rights.

Other delays resulted from, and compromises were required by, sharp differences over the inclusion or scope of particular rights. A majority of states were concerned, or were more concerned, with values reflecting their struggle against colonialism but not included in the Universal Declaration and not previously part of the accepted human rights ideology. They insisted that both covenants include the right of all peoples to self-determination as well as to "economic self-determination," to "sovereignty" over their resources.[15] Western states resisted, arguing that both are at best rights of a "people" not of any individual, surely not—like human rights generally—rights of individuals against their own society. They argued, too, that the content of these norms was highly uncertain and controversial.* The argument did not prevail, and identical provisions on self-determination now head both covenants. Also included in the Covenant on Civil and Political Rights were other, less controversial rights not mentioned in the Declaration—freedom from imprisonment for debt, rights of children, and of minorities (Articles 11, 24, 27). That Covenant also prohibits propaganda for war and incitement to national, racial, or religious hatred (Article 20). Some rights included in the Declaration were substantially elaborated. On the other hand, the right to enjoy private property, included in the Declaration, was finally omitted from the covenants.[16] Much time was also spent in the attempt to bridge the

---

*Although self-determination is now an accepted political, perhaps even legal, principle, its only agreed content is to bar white, European colonialism in Africa and Asia. It did not mean a right for Biafra to secede from Nigeria. It does not necessarily honor the present population's wishes or assure the people a bona fide expression of their self-determination. Compare the attack on British control of Gibraltar despite popular support with West Irian's incorporation into Indonesia or the disposition of the western Sahara. It does not preclude Soviet "influence" in East Europe. Self-determination apparently does not imply domestic democracy or representative government.

demand of some states for effective means to enforce the covenants and the insistence of others on the "sovereignty" of states and resistance to international scrutiny and "intrusion."[17]

In sum, and in general, the international law of human rights developed by the two covenants parallels the Universal Declaration and provides protections like those in the constitutions and laws of enlightened democratic-liberal countries as well as the promises of socialist and "welfare" constitutions.[18] Before, during, and since the negotiation of these two major covenants, the UN system also promoted specialized declarations and conventions—on genocide, on the status of refugees and stateless persons, on the rights of women, and on the elimination of all forms of racial discrimination.[19] These emphasize, extend, and supplement the protections afforded by the principal covenants. They have also made it possible to "extract" legal obligations on these particular subjects from governments not prepared to adhere to all the obligations of the general covenants.

How much law various covenants and conventions have made depends, of course, on the number of adherences to them. As of January 1, 1978, the Genocide Convention had eighty-two parties, the Convention on the Elimination of All Forms of Racial Discrimination ninety-seven, the Convention on Political Rights of Women eighty-two, and the Convention on the Status of Refugees sixty-nine.[20] Late in 1975, the Covenant on Political and Civil Rights and the Covenant on Economic and Social Rights obtained the adherences necessary to bring them into effect, and adherences have continued to "trickle" in. (As of early 1978, the former had forty-six, the latter forty-eight, adherences.) It matters, of course, whether covenants are accepted by populous nations or by those with small populations; whether the states that adhere are states more or less disposed to comply with their undertakings; or, on the other hand, whether some who have not adhered might nonetheless practice what the conventions require. (As to each of these conventions, some adherences are subject to reservations of greater or less significance.)

The "amount" of international human rights law, however, might be greater than these statistics suggest. It has been argued that by now the Universal Declaration, other declarations, conventions, resolutions, and practices have given specific content to the obligations of the UN Charter (to which all states are party) or have created a customary law of human rights binding on all states, at least as regards some norms.[21] Perhaps, then, genocide, racial discrimination, torture, and denial of fundamental fairness in criminal trials are violations of international law even if committed by states not party to any human rights convention.[22]

Enforcing Human Rights Obligations

The covenants and conventions, and the international human rights movement generally, struggled hard and long with means and methods for executing the new human rights law.

International law has generally been defensive about "law enforcement." There being no world government or other institutions with an effective executive arm, the very character of international law as "law" has been questioned, and some have reduced it to "exhortation," "voluntarism," and "moral imperative." Students of the international system have explained that there is in fact "horizontal enforcement": a state that is the victim of a violation will usually react in some relevant and appropriate way, for example, by retaliation; the expectation that the victim would react tends to deter violations. More important, these students insist, what matters is not whether law is "enforced" but whether it is observed.[23] Governments are impelled to observe international law because it is in their interest to do so, from a wish to maintain order, to keep the norms alive, to have the advantages of law they desire, and to avoid the hostile reactions of the victim and other adverse consequences of violations. As a result, "almost all nations observe almost all principles of international law and almost all of their obligations almost all of the time."[24]

In principle, the international law of human rights benefits from the same forces that induce compliance with international law generally: a human rights treaty gives each party the right to demand compliance by others and to react appropriately to violations.[25] But in contrast to other international law, in international human rights law it is not another state that is the victim of a violation of a multilateral human rights convention, but individual citizens of the violating state itself; it could not be assumed, therefore, that other states would respond to violations. That and other special qualities of human rights law have suggested additional methods of implementation. Some conventions provide special bodies before which one party may complain of another, for example, the Convention on the Elimination of All Forms of Racial Discrimination and an optional provision in the Covenant on Civil and Political Rights.[26] Because human rights obligations are essentially for the benefit of individuals, some conventions contain provisions—in most instances they are optional—whereby a state agrees that a designated body may receive and pursue complaints from individual "victims" or from nongovernmental organizations on their behalf.[27] There is some inducement to comply with human rights undertakings when a state has to report on its compliance, as the principal conventions require.[28] In a still-fledgling development, the Subcommission on Discrimination of the UN Human Rights Commission may receive and pursue communications that "appear to reveal a consistent pattern of gross and reliably attested violations," even in states that are party to no human rights agreements at all (other than the provisions of the UN Charter).[29] There has been a sustained (though yet unsuccessful) drive to establish a UN high commissioner for human rights to serve as a kind of world "ombudsman." And intergovernmental as well as nongovernmental organizations, communications media, and concerned individuals have sought to publicize violations, with a view to exerting pressure on the violating government to undo or discontinue them and to deter future violations.[30]

Regional Law

There is also regional human rights law—international law for its particular members, not designed to be universal. In principle, regional human rights covenants might supplement universal agreements, but they may substitute for them and have other purposes as well. States not prepared to adhere to all the provisions of the universal agreements, or to enter into such agreements "with all comers," might be willing to assume some or all of those obligations with states with whom they have much else in common or other special relations. Regional human rights movements may also serve a general cause of political integration and other local ends. The countries of Western Europe doubtless believed that international human rights obligations were not necessary for them, since their national legal systems were generally satisfactory. But as part of the "Europeanization" of the region, they also sought to declare their devotion to human rights as a hallmark of their common values; they sought an additional area for cooperation, one that would not require great disturbance of existing national institutions; and they wished to contribute to human rights everywhere by making active identification with them. Friendly relations among them dispelled any fear that the obligations undertaken or the institutions established for implementing them would be abused to harass one another.

Hence, as the most notable example, the European human rights system. By its convention and supplementary protocols, Western Europe established a European law of political-civil rights and a complex of institutions and procedures to give it effect, providing for both state and private complaints and possible considerations by the Commission on Human Rights, by the Committee of Ministers, and by a Court of Human Rights. The European Convention and its protocols protect most, but not all, of the rights included in the UN Covenant on Civil and Political Rights, with variations; the First Protocol also recognized the right to an education (which is in the UN

Covenant on Economic, Social and Cultural Rights). Unlike the UN Covenant, the European system protects the right to property ("the peaceful enjoyment of one's possessions," First Protocol, Article 1) and the right not to be expelled from one's country of nationality (Fourth Protocol, Article 3); and forbids the collective expulsion of aliens (Fourth Protocol, Article 4).[31]

It is perhaps paradoxical but not surprising that the area of the world in least need of international support for human rights has produced the most impressive international system. It was not, in fact, idle or merely cosmetic European institutions that stood out against Greek unlawful detentions, torture, and political repression during the rule of "the Colonels." These institutions have called Great Britain to account for tolerating torture and unlawful detention in Northern Ireland. Less dramatic cases have involved challenges to criminal procedures and punishment and to limitations on freedom of expression and publication and on the scope of trade union freedom; they have involved challenges to military discipline, vagrancy legislation, and compulsory education laws. (But there have also been thousands of complaints that have been ruled "inadmissible" and not pursued.) A jurisprudence of substantive law and of procedure has been growing for European use and for example to others.

Different, though analogous, influences supported regional human rights activities in Latin America, with both the law and institutions there developed bearing marks characteristic of the region. The American Convention (in force as of July 1978) contains a complete catalog of political-civil rights corresponding to the UN Covenant on Civil and Political Rights (to which Latin American states made important contributions), but it also has variations of some significance. Unlike the UN covenants, for example, it protects private property.[32] In regard to economic, social, and cultural rights, however, it was modest and sober. The chapter dealing with them consists of a single article, headed "Progressive Development":

> The States Parties undertake to adopt measures, both internally and through international cooperation, especially those of an economic and technical nature, with a view to achieving progressively, by legislation or other appropriate means, the full realization of the rights implicit in the economic, social, educational, scientific, and cultural standards set forth in the Charter of the Organization of American States as amended by the Protocol of Buenos Aires [Article 26].

Latin American institutions for promoting human rights are promising, although less developed than those of Europe. Latin American states are perhaps more reluctant than the Europeans to submit to criticism by neighboring governments, especially with the "radicalization" of some societies and governments in the region. But they have been willing, in principle, to accept scrutiny by regional institutions of complaints from their inhabitants. These regional institutions and representatives show less self-restraint and caution in probing and pursuing charges of human rights violations.[33]

Other regions—Africa, the Muslim world—have also felt challenged to attend to human rights, but to date they have produced no significant human rights law or institutions.[34]

The Condition of the Law Today

The international law of human rights is a remarkable achievement, accomplished in only thirty years, by a political system in flux, of growing complexity, and deeply divided in relevant ideology. It has imposed international legal limitations on governments that knew no effective legal limitations in their domestic constitutional systems, and it has confirmed and supplemented the limitations on governments that did. The law dealing with civil-political rights sets high standards. Even the limitations and derogations permitted by the conventions are largely those that are inevitable and that modify even the most libertarian national constitutions and laws; they are not intrinsically destructive of human rights, and any abuse of them can be challenged as a violation of the convention. If, in some instances, conflicting rights, or conflict between rights and some other social good, lead to dispositions in international law different from those approved, say, by U.S. constitutional law, the international answer is not necessarily inferior or inadequate. If the law of economic-social rights is largely aspiration, it is no more so than is in the nature of these rights, no more so than is true of similar provisions in national constitutions and laws.

But if the normative content of the law does not leave overmuch to be desired, one must wish for wider acceptance of and greater compliance with it. Only the Genocide Convention and the Convention on the Elimination of All Forms of Racial Discrimination have been adhered to by a majority of states. States perhaps saw their adherence to the former as dissociating them from Hitler's unspeakable horrors. Wide adherences to the latter convention are a tribute to the success of the Asian-African bloc in rendering racial discrimination a major "crime" in contemporary international society, and to their ability to persuade or shame other powers, big and small, into adhering to this convention. Many states that have adhered doubtless believed that it would have no serious application for them, if only because, despite its general language, its effective target is white discrimination against blacks. Other major conventions—notably the International Covenant on Civil and Political Rights and the Covenant on Economic, Social and Cultural Rights—have far fewer adherences, and influential states—including, to our discredit, the United States—are among the missing. And some adherences may be cynical, for with inadequate "enforcement," a state can adhere in order to obtain international or domestic political advantage, without incurring any effective limitations.*

---

*Accusations of such cynicism were leveled by some Americans at the USSR when it adhered to the UN Covenant on Civil and Political Rights and the Convention on the Elimination of All Forms of Racial Discrimination. It was noted that the Soviet Union

The principal weakness of the international law of human rights is the inadequacy of its "enforcement." The UN has addressed itself in particular to racism, and its failures to end apartheid to date speak to the difficulty of eradicating even an egregious violation that is fundamental national policy. As regards other violations elsewhere, neither the general means of "enforcement" of international law by "sanctions" between parties to an agreement, nor the special ones proposed to induce compliance with human rights law, have been markedly successful to date. Although the deterrent influence of human rights law and institutions cannot be proved or measured, obviously deterrence was not effective wherever violations occur. There is little "horizontal," state-to-state enforcement. Direct complaint between states party to a convention is theoretically possible but rare.[35] The principal human rights conventions do not give the International Court of Justice compulsory jurisdiction to resolve disputes arising under them. A clause to that effect is included in the Convention on the Elimination of All Forms of Racial Discrimination (Article 22), but many states have entered reservations refusing to submit to it. States could go to the court by mutual agreement in a particular instance (without advance general agreement to do so), but that too seems unlikely to happen here. Unilateral reporting by states to the UN or to a special body apparently does not deter violations and improve performance, perhaps because the reports tend to be self-serving and evasive and have not been effectively scrutinized. Complaint by one state against another before a special committee is contemplated by some conventions, but in the principal agreement—the Covenant on Civil and Political Rights—submission to such complaint is optional; to date, only six states have agreed to do it.[37]

The most direct, and some believe the most promising,

has not accepted the optional provisions or the optional protocol submitting to complaints, and has made a reservation to the clause in the Racial Discrimination Convention accepting the jurisdiction of the International Court of Justice.[36]

"enforcement" procedures are those that entail impartial considerations of complaints from victims of alleged violations or from organizations on their behalf.* Only one-third of the states that have adhered to the Covenant on Political and Civil Rights have agreed also, by optional protocol, to submit to such complaints.[38] The Human Rights Committee created by the Covenant has begun its work and will consider both state complaints against those few states that have submitted to it as well as private complaints against states party to the Protocol; much will hang on its effectiveness in undoing or deterring violations and building an effective jurisprudence. The procedure of the UN Sub-Commission on Discrimination (unrelated to any convention) for hearing complaints of "a consistent pattern of gross and reliably attested violations"[39] is still young, and its future still uncertain. The proposal for a high commissioner is on the shelf, frustrated once again in 1977. And though international law of human rights might influence governmental behavior by its existence alone (even without any enforcement machinery), though general international awareness may have deterrent effect, and though states may respect human rights under constraint of domestic forces and domestic law, these surely are not effective enough, for the condition of human rights, we know, is less than happy in many countries of the world.

_____

*The politics of implementation have proved different from what had been anticipated. The early assumption that states might be prepared to scrutinize other states and be scrutinized by them was still reflected in earlier conventions; it was then assumed also that they would be far more reluctant to submit to international scrutiny of complaints by their own citizens. Thus state scrutiny was included in the Convention on the Elimination of All Forms of Racial Discrimination, and in fact it has apparently not deterred adherence, perhaps because pressures upon states to adhere to that convention were strong, perhaps because states willing to join did not fear accusation. Private complaint was also provided in the Convention but made optional, and only a few states have submitted to it. The International Covenant on Civil and Political Rights also included provision for state-to-state complaint, but it was made optional, and submission to private complaints was not even included in the Covenant but was relegated to a separate optional protocol. In fact, however, to date, more states have submitted to private complaints than to interstate scrutiny. Obviously, then, some states that are willing to have their citizens' complaints scrutinized are still reluctant to be accused by other governments and have human rights trouble their diplomatic relations.

Disappointed Expectations

There are, in my view, several reasons why the expectations from the international law of human rights and the human rights movement generally have not been better realized. The international law was designed to supply national deficiencies, but many of the reasons why national law is inadequate in many countries militate also against international law's being effective there; nations not willing and able of their own accord to respect and promote human rights at home are also not eager to assume and observe international obligations or to respond to other international influences to do so.

Even today in many countries there is still no deep commitment to human rights. Surely there is no essential consensus on the importance of human rights, on which rights are "fundamental," on priorities among competing rights or between rights and other public goods. The comparison of political groupings of states (Chapter 2) suggests fundamental differences not conducive to universal international law. In many societies, we saw, political-civil rights in particular are seen as a luxury, even as an obstacle to the realization of other goals, to state building, stability, socialism, and economic and social development. In some, the guiding principle is revolution and revolutionary justice (whether of the Left, the Right, or some other), not the "tired liberalism" of the Universal Declaration. In some countries, e.g., the Republic of South Africa, violations of human rights are essential national policy, which does not respond to international law and other likely international pressures.

Also disappointed has been the human rights movement's assumption that states generally accepted that human rights everywhere were everyone's business and were prepared, or might be persuaded, to accept external scrutiny of their behavior in regard to individual rights and to submit to an international law of human rights. The advantages to the national interest from assuming this kind of international obligation have been small, and the pressures to do so have generally not been too difficult to resist. Even some countries with respectable attitudes to human rights at home—such as the United States—have been unwilling to assume international obligations about them and have resisted having their behavior scrutinized by others who may have political or other ulterior motives for criticizing them. Surely, closed societies, which are most in need of improvement, are also most resistant to international inducements to improve.

Least anticipated was the unwillingness of states to scrutinize the behavior of others; without that scrutiny, even when legal obligations are assumed, they seem light and empty obligations, and the usual inducements to comply with them are tenuous. An international law of human rights implies that how a state party to an agreement treats its own inhabitants is of proper and legitimate concern to the other parties, but governments have not yet generally assimilated that implication. Other states are the promisees of human rights undertakings, but they are not the real beneficiaries; and since human rights are not a top value, since violations of human rights in other countries are not seen as of great national moment, scrutiny by one state of another has tended to be seen by both as officious meddling, threatening relations between them. States have thus been reluctant to expend much political capital and diplomatic goodwill on account of them. Governments have concerned themselves strongly for human rights elsewhere only when their concern coincided with other national interests or served other political ends, for example, India's "humanitarian intervention" at the creation of Bangladesh.

The disappointed expectations of the human rights movement explain the disappointing results—in the number of adherences to major conventions, in the weakness of enforcement machinery, and above all, of course, in failure to improve the condition of human rights in many countries. They explain, too, the condition of the international human rights movement itself in today's international political system. The international human rights movement was begun and led by Western states. The communist states resisted it, perhaps because they strongly resisted international "penetration" of their societies in any form, perhaps because individual human rights were essentially antithetical to Marxist-Leninist doctrine. Human rights, however, had political and rhetorical appeal, and communist states could not afford to reject it outright. Instead they sought to convert the movement to "socialist principles," to give it a socioeconomic emphasis. Later adherence by the communist world to the UN agreements and declarations apparently did not reflect or bring a radical change in ideology or commitment. The rise of the Third World to political influence, particularly in the UN, gave it sufficient independence so that its members did not have to join the East-West battle on the old turf, although if pressed most of them would probably lean to the socialist view. Unlike the communist states, the Third World had an important interest in the international human rights movement to support their strong determination to eliminate the remains of white racism in southern Africa, but in their own countries many of the Third World states have not been deeply interested in individual human rights, not even in economic-social rights. Their real interest is in the economic development of the society as a whole and in the "equalization" of states, and the human rights linkage is essentially a means to those ends. They have seized the human rights mantle also for the cause of "anti-economic imperialism" and the New International Economic Order—hence for the right to "economic self-determination" at the head of both UN covenants. (In 1977 they had the UN General Assembly formally affirm that link and the "priority" of economic-social rights and of collective rights, of the rights of "the people," against outsiders rather than of the individual against his own government.)[40] Their emphasis has been not on the individual, not even on the economic and social rights of living individuals, but on development, on "gross national product" and "per capita income," with the rights of individuals an indirect beneficiary and a more distant prospect.

Superficial commitment to human rights, lack of consensus, and reluctance to submit to and to exercise international scrutiny have also contributed to a general "politicization" of the international law of human rights and of the international institutions that deal with them. The condition of human rights is judged not by impartial judicial tribunals applying "neutral principles," but by political bodies that subordinate human rights to other political interests. States have tended to charge violations only by a few states with which their relations are otherwise unfriendly. Political blocs have resisted airing of accusations against one of their members or have united against a political enemy. Violations in some parts of the world have not even been discussed. Sometimes complaints have been fabricated, exaggerated, or otherwise distorted. In the principal political organs like the UN General Assembly, and even in specialized human rights bodies, politicization has meant, for example, overlooking charges of human rights violation against the USSR, the Arab states, or Uganda, while exaggerating those of Israel; compromising universal rejection of racism by an incredible resolution condemning Zionism as racism; some states agreeing to overlook human rights violations in exchange for political support on other issues;[41] refusing to deal seriously with the implications for human rights of political terrorism; threatening nongovernmental organizations that embarrass powerful states.[42] On the other hand, even when a complaint is well founded, the human rights element in the controversy has often been subordinated, and the accused state has been unlikely to heed it.

Politicization has affected even the rights that particularly interested the majority—self-determination and freedom from racial discrimination. Self-determination, we have seen, has been applied less than impartially.[43] Interest in freedom from racial discrimination has been acute where whites discriminate against blacks, as in South Africa; there is less concern where Africans discriminate against Asians, as in Uganda; and there is virtual indifference about discrimination against other kinds of groups, such as tribes or ethnic and religious communities. The cause of human rights has also not been served when its mantle is invoked for other causes, even worthy causes like "economic self-determination." Surely human rights are distorted and abused when states assert a right to "freedom from information," to deny their people access to information and knowledge, ostensibly in order to preserve their cultural purity and traditional values.[44]

New Momentum

The condition of human rights in most parts of the world remains less than happy, yet the mood of disappointment and resignation that had hung over the international human rights movement lifted in the 1970s, and gave way to renewed determination and momentum.

The reasons for the change in mood are several, and complicated. The prospects for human rights have improved in Spain and Portugal, where established autarchies were replaced by systems promising parliamentary democracy; in Greece, libertarian fortunes flourished again; India, the world's most populous democracy and a possible model for the democratic way in the Third World, voted out two years of repression. At Helsinki, when the Soviet Union sought political ratification of the status quo in Eastern Europe and increased East-West trade, Western states exacted human rights commitments in exchange. Emboldened dissidents, particularly in communist countries, invited and received support from Western governments. Communist parties and leaders in Western Europe spoke out for greater individual freedom. The UN and the Organization of American States responded to charges of torture and repression on the part of some regimes that were otherwise unpopular (e.g., Chile), thus giving new scope and new hope to UN efforts, notably those of the UN Human Rights Commission. In 1977 the African states, in order to forestall discussion by the General Assembly, agreed to request an investigation by the UN Human Rights Commission of alleged atrocities in Uganda.[45] To the surprise of many, the International Covenant on Civil and Political Rights and its protocol, as well as the Covenant on Economic and Social Rights, came into effect, and the number of adherents continued to grow, steadily if slowly. The Human Rights Committee established by the Civil and Political Rights Covenant was organized and began its work.

In the 1970s the Universal Declaration achieved the universality denied it at birth; that is, the communist bloc (which had abstained in 1948) accepted it. In 1973 the Soviet Union adhered to the two international covenants deriving from the Declaration, not only to the Covenant on Economic, Social and Cultural Rights (which responds to socialist ideas) but also to the Covenant on Civil and Political rights (which the West values). (Communist adherence, indeed, helped supply the number of adherences necessary to bring the two covenants into effect.) In 1975 at Helsinki, in the Final Act of the Conference on Security and Cooperation in Europe, the Soviet Union and its allies accepted respect for human rights as a "principle guiding relations between participating states" and declared expressly that they "will act in conformity with" the Universal Declaration and will comply with the international human rights covenants by which they may be bound, including specifically the International Covenants.

Communist adherence to the norms and institutions of the international human rights movement hardly proves a sudden and radical conversion to Western ideas. Although the international norms are now reflected in governmental rhetoric (and in the 1977 constitution of the USSR), there is no evidence that Soviet acceptance of them ushered in any substantial change in the condition of human rights in the communist countries; even the specific and limited commitments in "Basket Three" of the Final Act at Helsinki have received only modest and grudging implementation. The communist states will doubtless justify their performance by insisting on their own interpretation of the documents, including the derogation provisions and "loopholes," and on their versions of fact. But the communist countries doubtless realized that by making these political and legal commitments, they opened themselves to both domestic and international pressures to improve their human rights performance. Whatever advantages they saw from adhering, whatever other reasons impelled them to make these commitments and invite these additional pressures, may well require also that they in fact ameliorate the condition of human rights in their countries and thereby substantially reduce the deficiencies in the human rights consensus.

The Third World, including the many states that did not yet exist when the Universal Declaration was adopted, has also seen fit to come under its banner and indeed to assert its binding quality. Third World states are also adhering to the international covenants in a steady "trickle." Although, when acting together, they have the votes in international organizations to assert their own interpretations and "priorities" and to resist international criticism and pressure about human rights, they have joined the human rights movement and responded to its appealing rhetoric. That, and the legal commitments by Third World states that have adhered to the covenant, also generate pressure on Third World countries to improve their own performance at home, and narrow the gap between domestic performance and the consensus reflected in the international documents. The Third World also has its own human rights priorities, in its determination to end colonialism and white racism in southern Africa, and many Third World states realize that the wide international support it seeks for that struggle will be more forthcoming if the human rights consensus generally is wider and stronger.

The United States and International Human Rights

Perhaps the strongest inspiration and momentum have come from changing attitudes by the United States. Americans, of course, take pride in their contribution to the international human rights movement. We see respect for individual rights as our national hallmark and an example to the world, and in fact, despite glaring exceptions and occasional lapses, human rights are respected in the United States as never before and to a greater degree than in almost all other countries.[46] The Constitution and many laws promote such rights, and public as well as nongovernmental institutions are alert against their violation.

Americans can properly also claim a substantial part in launching the ideas of human rights upon the world and giving them our own imprint, and our Constitution has been a principal inspiration and model for others. The United States has been second to no other major country in launching the international effort to establish, promote, and maintain human rights. American traditions and ideas helped to give it shape and particular content, and American predispositions were prominent in making human rights a matter of international political concern. Even before 1945, U.S. officials and nongovernmental organizations stressed the relevance of human rights to international peace and to other common international purposes, and insisted that international law and institutions to protect such rights were proper and necessary; their efforts helped enshrine human rights in the UN Charter and establish the Human Rights Commission. The United States—represented by Eleanor Roosevelt—led in the creation of the classic document of contemporary human rights—the Universal Declaration of Human Rights—and U.S. representatives were important participants in the preparation of the various covenants and conventions. American nongovernmental organizations have been most active in monitoring the human rights behavior of states and the performance of international institutions.

The commitment of the U.S. government to international human rights, however, has been less than wholehearted, and our participation has not been distinguished. World War II, we know, joined the "idealists" and the "realists" in government in support of the war effort and in giving it idealistic aims, and they remained joined in planning for the postwar period, at Nuremberg, in the preparation of the peace treaties, in occupation policy, in the preparation of the UN Charter, all of which included dedication to promoting human rights. After the glow of victory and the "spirit of the United Nations" waned, however, there was a bifurcation within governments, including our own. The "human rights contingent" remained but went its way; and the Universal Declaration (the handiwork of Eleanor Roosevelt, not of Dean Acheson), the Genocide Convention, the covenants, and the other conventions followed. The "realists"—the traditional diplomats—concerned themselves with other important things: security, alignments, bases, trade. Inevitably, the realists dominated. Doubtless, many of them considered the preoccupation of their colleagues with human rights, welfare, and related subjects as unsophisticated and officious; but they were not disposed to challenge it as long as it remained on the plane of rhetoric or of law that was not adhered to or actively enforced. That human rights remained generally on an international "byway" and did not become the preoccupation of "real diplomats" may explain the common impression that international human rights have been all rhetoric and exhortation. It is perhaps not surprising that after thirty years of internationalization, government spokesmen still commonly feel, and sometimes say, that what a country does to its own inhabitants is its own business.

As a result, the United States has been, one might say, not a pillar of the church of international human rights, but a flying buttress, supporting it from the outside. We have seen international human rights as for others only. Our respect for human rights, we believe, already surpasses any acceptable international standard; the need is to bring the blessings of our liberties to others. Even when Americans are urging their government to adhere to some international human rights agreement (or when the executive is seeking the Senate's consent to it, as the Constitution requires), they feel obliged to insist that our adherence would entail no change in our law, institutions, or practices; the United States should ratify only to encourage others and to give us the right to intervene in support of human rights in countries where such intervention is needed. Even the victims of human rights violations in this country have not seriously sought international protection nor urged U.S. participation in international programs out of sympathy with victims elsewhere. (The domestic civil rights movement in the United States and our foreign policy on human rights have remained discrete and unrelated.)

Because we believe that human rights in the United States need no international support; because we do not think we have anything to learn in human rights from others and we even fear dilution or "contamination" from them; because, though we continue to assert that human rights are everybody's business, we make an exception where those of our own citizens are concerned; because we have always remained in some measure "isolationist," especially resisting foreign "interference" here; because we fear that foreign scrutiny might bring subversion, distortion, or hostile propaganda—the United States has refused to be a full and equal participant in the international human rights program. Most glaringly, it has adhered to virtually no human rights agreement of any importance.[47] We alone of major powers have had the self-confidence to resist adhering to the Genocide Convention or the Convention on the Elimination of All Forms of Racial Discrimination. We have not adhered to the principal elements of the "International Bill of Rights"—the Covenant on Civil and Political Rights and the Covenant on Economic, Social and Cultural Rights—although the former is the most promising vehicle for strengthening our human values around the world. By contrast, the countries of Western Europe, with equally enlightened traditions and respectable performance at home, have a respectable record of adherences to universal agreements and have achieved as well an advanced regional human rights program.[48] Other governments, though they might recognize that the United States does well in human rights, even perhaps that it is "holier than they," have not responded to U.S. self-righteousness, even before Vietnam and Watergate made the validity of our pretensions less than obvious. Surely, the United States could have no influence to persuade others to subscribe to international human rights law and to other participation in the international human rights effort.

We have, indeed, sometimes recognized that the state of human rights elsewhere impinges on our foreign interests. In general, we believe that the world would be a better place, and U.S. interests in it would fare better, if other countries were more like us in respect for human rights. Human rights violations also bring particular disturbances to our foreign policy: in recent decades, Franco's Spain, the Greek colonels, repressive Turkish regimes, reactionary Portugal, the Philippines, or the Republic of Korea—all have been allies with which we have not been wholly comfortable. Abominations by trading partners like South Africa and Rhodesia have given rise to continued criticism from our citizens and from others. Massacres of alleged communists in Indonesia by a government that, from the U.S. point of view, was otherwise a great improvement over its predecessor, troubled both officials and citizens in this country. The Soviet government's maltreatment of Jews led senators to resist detente and most-favored-nation treatment for the USSR. Even Great Britain's troubles in Northern Ireland (which have deep human rights veins) have upset U.S. citizens and congressmen and troubled our special relationship with our closest ally. (In a different way, U.S. interests are affected when slavery and forced labor, child labor, and starvation wages produce goods that compete "unfairly" with U.S. products in world markets.)

In these and other instances, effective international protection fairly and vigorously applied would further U.S. interests. But the traditional attitude that human rights elsewhere are not really our business has been deeply rooted, and U.S.

policymakers, handicapped perhaps by our own nonparticipa-
tion, have not sought to build a strong, impartial, "apolitical"
international effort. They have occasionally resisted what they
considered an unwarranted attack (e.g., against Israel), but they
have not fought the politicization of human rights generally
and on all fronts, being less than wholly committed to the
international movement and unwilling to pay the political
price that the struggle might cost. Even when political interests
required it, the United States had to be "dragged" and was
prepared to sacrifice only a little, e.g., to meet Third World
demands for stronger pressure upon Rhodesia and South
Africa.

In sum, despite early interest and leadership, the international protection of human rights has been a kind of "white
man's burden," and the United States itself has remained
largely outside the international human rights program. That
has been for this country a peripheral aspect of its UN
activities, themselves increasingly peripheral, and at most
times conducted by officials peripheral to the seats of power
and the major concerns of foreign policy. Preoccupation with
human rights elsewhere, whether in a multilateral forum or
bilaterally, still tends to strike many of our policymakers as
meddling and as disturbing to friendly relations and international order. Surely, despite occasional rhetoric to contrary,
the protection of human rights elsewhere has not been an
integral plank in the foreign policy of the United States, high
among its foreign interests and to be pursued vigorously even at
substantial cost. It has not been the concern of presidents,
secretaries of state, and even of congressional leaders, except to
assure that United States involvement remained minimal and
"inexpensive."

In the 1970s changes appeared. Under pressure from
Congress, the executive branch became more aware of, and
more concerned with, violations of human rights elsewhere.[49]
Congress also enacted laws that would deny or reduce military
assistance and other foreign aid to governments that engaged in

"a consistent pattern of gross violations of internationally recognized human rights." Although executive resistance, and competing United States interests, tended at first to reduce the effectiveness of such measures,[50] the administration that took office in 1977 promised new attitudes. President Carter, Secretary of State Vance, and other officials spoke out vigorously in support of human rights and against human rights violations in other countries; they seemed prepared to consider human rights abroad an important national concern to be weighed seriously with other national interests in the formulation of national policy generally and toward particular countries. "Human rights officials" in the Department of State, introduced there pursuant to congressional mandate, made up a "constituency" for human rights, less resistant to congressional pressure. The new policy offered hope that the United States might move into the mainstream of the international human rights movement and lend its important weight, bilaterally as well as through international bodies, to improving the human rights condition. It promised to put human rights high on every international agenda, rendering them accepted daily fare in international relations.

The new U.S. preoccupation with human rights has not been universally welcomed even in the West, nor yet in the United States. Some saw it as evangelistic, moralistic intrusion in the domestic affairs of other states. Some feared that it would jeopardize alliances, trouble detente with the USSR, antagonize many other governments, disturb international relations, and damage U.S. interests everywhere. Some thought it might encourage dissidence and build up false hopes for U.S. military intervention. Some were concerned that it might make repressive regimes even more repressive.

Others, however, rose and responded to the new human rights "activism." They thought that the United States should proclaim its ideological commitment, speak out for freedom everywhere, identify with and support those who share its values; and should deny its alliance, its friendship, its largesse to those who reject them. They urged the United States to adhere to international covenants and participate fully in human rights agencies. They stressed that the West, having paid in valuable political coin for human rights commitments by the USSR and its bloc at Helsinki, should now keep human rights as a central item on the East-West agenda. Since the whole world has made the commitment to civil and political rights (in the Universal Declaration and in the Covenant), the West should now strive to assure that these authentic libertarian, humanitarian values are not distorted or diluted.

It remains to be seen whether the new U.S. attitudes will last and their reach and influence extended. It remains to be seen whether they will be effective to depoliticize and strengthen the human rights movement and, above all, ameliorate the condition of human rights in various countries.

Prospect

The history of the international movement to date does not demonstrate that human rights are not valuable or important, only that to advance them will be more difficult than some had believed or hoped. In retrospect, surely, there was never any reason to expect universal agreement on their philosophical and political doctrine, or rapid radical conversion to them in countries where they were not embedded in the cultural consciousness and conscience. If there were ready, wide, and deep agreement on human rights, they would have been promoted and protected in every country through domestic institutions, and there would have been little need for an international human rights movement. In fact, instead of despair, one might feel amazement and encouragement at even the modest progress in human rights and in international involvement, at the continuing vitality of the international human rights program. It is instructive and encouraging that countries with different traditions and ideologies and different economic, social, and political situations should nonetheless accept a common code of human rights if only in principle and in aspiration, and devote tremendous resources and energies to the problems of realizing human rights.

Much that I have described might change dramatically. With radical political change, respect for human rights might come to some countries and disappear from others. Although a deep consensus on the content and value of human rights cannot come overnight, although attitudes that have politicized the human rights movement cannot be quickly transformed, particular political impulses that have troubled the international program could disappear suddenly. A settlement in the Middle East, for example, would make it easier for international organs to deal with human rights issues in that area, perhaps also in Eastern Europe, on their merits; it would weaken the baneful influence of Soviet-Arab cooperation and other alignments hostile to international scrutiny, and it would reduce the politicization of human rights generally. Resolutions in Namibia and Rhodesia and other changes in southern Africa might dilute the UN concentration on antiblack discrimination and encourage attention to other human rights violations. Or, to the contrary, new tensions— among the big powers, in particular regions, or within countries—might set back human rights and the efforts to protect them.

Radical transformation, however, cannot be anticipated. Immediately, one must assume more of the same—in human rights around the world, in the UN, in international protection. One must assume that the original expectations and hopes will not fare dramatically better in the near future than they have until now. Like other hopes for essential international improvement that bloomed in the wake of World War II, the human rights movement will have to reexamine assumptions and expectations and respond to the lessons to be learned.

One of these is patience: the international system has been in operation for only thirty years, after a long human history of different attitudes and expectations. Other lessons suggest things to be done. If one seeks universal law, one had better work at building the consensus necessary to support it and the political attitudes necessary to maintain it; there is need for cooperation and comparative learning and teaching by officials, scholars, and citizens. If existing inducements to undertake and observe human rights obligations are in-adequate, they must be strengthened and others developed. Since, for example, nations that have adhered to covenants or supported declarations cannot lightly refuse to report on their compliance, one might develop effective scrutiny of these reports. It has been suggested that transnational professional organizations—of trade unions, writers, scientists, doctors, or lawyers—might achieve effective entry into various closed countries and more effective influence for human rights there. I have wondered whether often-frustrated efforts to create a commissioner of human rights might not be advanced if he began as a commissioner for the elimination of racial discrimination, a subject as to which states have gone farthest in accepting international scrutiny.[51] A "human rights bloc" of states might lead a campaign to depoliticize human rights, so that states might pursue the cause of human rights without jeopardy to their international relations, indeed, with benefit to them and to other international business. If dominant political influences within the United Nations continue to serve human rights badly, the cause of human rights (and the cause of the UN) might require diverting some or much of the human rights program to more hospitable channels. Addi-tional regional bodies can perhaps be persuaded to take on the task, if only to keep regional "dirty laundry" from being flaunted before a wide, less friendly public. If our hopes are to do better during the next thirty years, the United States must join the human rights movement and concern itself in good faith, impartially, with the condition of human rights everywhere. (Might the lesson of thirty years be that for the United States, military alliances, friendships, and even trade partnerships are secure only with countries that share our values, not the least our care for human rights?) If governments resist and resent external scrutiny and criticism, perhaps they can be persuaded by private dialogue and assistance to improve their laws and institutions.

Human rights, I believe, will continue to be a staple of international political life. The entire international political system—First, Second, and Third Worlds—has accepted the commitment to human rights and has agreed in principle on what they entail. Virtually every state is party to the obligations of the UN Charter and has accepted the Universal Declaration; many are party to specific covenants and conventions. At Helsinki, in the Conference on Security and Cooperation in Europe, participants agreed that respect for human rights (including specifically conformity with the Universal Declaration and with international agreements to which they are party) is one of the "principles guiding relations" among participating states. As a result, the human rights of all persons everywhere are of international concern, no longer "a matter essentially within the domestic jurisdiction" of any state.[52] It is not intervention or other improper interference for international organizations to monitor compliance with these commitments; or for one party to an agreement to call another to account by peaceful diplomatic means for failure to abide by its commitments; or for one state, if it so desires, to take another's human rights record into account in determining the warmth of their relations, the level of friendliness, trade, aid, or other largesse.

Human rights, as they have been, will be deeply implicated in the realities of international politics. Virtually every government has repeatedly invoked international human rights against some other government. Only Ian Smith of Rhodesia insists that the world is interfering in internal affairs there; the government of South Africa is virtually alone in believing that apartheid is no one else's business. A majority of the UN has voted to condemn several other countries and has approved intercession against any "consistent pattern of gross violations." At Helsinki, the West gave consideration of value in exchange for human rights commitments and established machinery for following up on this exchange. Almost all countries agree on, insist on, international human rights scrutiny in some cases for some purposes; governments differ only as to which violators of which rights they will call to account. The Third World calls on all to attend to hunger, colonialism, and racism everywhere; others will feel entitled to add to this human rights agenda and ask for an end to massacres, torture, unwarranted detention, fake trials, and repression. And though monitoring of human rights by international bodies is doubtless to be preferred, when such monitoring is absent or ineffective, it will inevitably invite scrutiny and judgment by nongovernmental organizations and the press and by particular governments.

The United States has made human rights an element in its foreign policy, asserting the right to call violators to public account, linking important national decisions (on aid, trade, arms sales) to the condition of individual rights in different countries. Its policies will require dialogue—with communist countries, with the Third World, as well as with Western allies. (At home there will have to be understanding between the executive branch and Congress and among the people.)

The USSR and other communist nations in Europe have donned the human rights mantle and have committed themselves to abide by all the rights articulated in the Universal Declaration and to be guided by them in relations with other nations participating in Helsinki.* Surely the United States is entitled to talk human rights to them. But we have to be clear in our own minds and attempt to persuade them that human rights are not being used as a "cold war weapon," that our concern is only to improve the condition of human rights

---

*The 1977 constitution of the USSR declares that the USSR's relations with other states are based on observance of enumerated principles (taken from the Helsinki Final Act), including expressly "respect for human rights and fundamental freedoms" (Article 29).

everywhere. We may believe that the communist system is not an authentic democracy and that it does not satisfy the human rights of individuals to authentic participation in government, but we recognize that "the communist system is not negotiable," and that it is not our purpose to subvert it. The communist world has asserted, has enshrined in its constitutions, and accepted in international undertakings that all other human rights, as reflected in the Universal Declaration, are consistent with communism. It will surely agree that nothing in communist theory or in "Soviet legality" requires or justifies torture or other mistreatment, extended detention, police harassment and "politicized" justice, anti-Semitism and other invidious ethnic discriminations, and denial of freedom of expression and of movement.

The Third World has not only accepted the Universal Declaration, but it has also invoked it and other international human rights documents in demanding aid against hunger and racism; if against these, we might ask, why not also universal action against massacre and mass expulsion, torture and illegal detention? If against South Africa and Chile, why not against Burundi, Equatorial Guinea and Uganda, Cambodia and Indonesia, the Philippines, Korea, and Brazil— if alleged atrocities are found true? If the United States is taken to task by the Third World for its economic and racial inadequacies, why not China and the Soviet Union for their flagrant human rights deficiencies?

Dialogue, of course, is a two-way exchange. We can expect to hear not only charges of "moral imperialism," but also reminders of our own human rights deficiencies as well as our international failures (including our dismal record of non-adherence to international human rights conventions). Even men and women of goodwill and sympathy will tell us that if political-civil rights are crucial, if indeed they distinguish the United States from many other societies, Americans have to learn more about these values themselves and about their intimate relation to economic and social rights. We will be charged with being "ethnocentric," with thinking our way is the only way, with failing to distinguish the essential from the peripheral, the universal from the idiosyncratic, the abiding from the transitory, the authentically human in human rights ideology from the particular forms that are specific to the West. We will be reminded that we have developed and refined our own conceptions and realized them only slowly during two hundred years. We have been up from slavery only a hundred years, and other forms of invidious discrimination are still being slowly worn away. We have long thought that participation in democratic representative government is a right, but we have been slow in making that right a universal human right. In our own day, we have known too well the tensions between liberty and order. We continue to redefine the proper domain of government and the sacrosanct autonomy of the individual; we redefine the balance between the legitimate demands of majorities and the hard-core immunities of minorities and individuals; and we redefine how much of the present we may sacrifice to the future, as well as the extent to which we may mortgage our descendants for our needs.

It is important that we in the United States also recognize where we have been, where we stand, and where we are going, as regards the rights others have preferred—economic and social rights. Here, too, we have reexamined and abandoned old rights and have enshrined new rights undreamed of only a few years ago. We have finally recognized that in economic matters, laissez-faire may look like liberty but often invites economic aggression, and that it must bow to regulation for the common welfare. We now believe that democratic government is not only "watchdog" but also has responsibilities for common, individual welfare; that taking from those who have (as by graduated, rational, fair income tax) to give to those who need (as by assuring to all the essentials of a life in dignity) is an essential of contemporary republican democracy. Have we not given near-constitutional status to the right to live and eat, to work and learn, and to be secure?[53]

But accepting the reminders of our own history and admitting the charges as to past and even present inadequacies, the United States is entitled to pursue the dialogue in the light of the contemporary values that all have accepted in our time. All agree that human rights include access to "basic human needs"—life, food, shelter, work, leisure, and education; they also include liberty and equality, equity and fairness, authentic participation in government, and individual autonomy and dignity. The United States and other Western democracies recognize the staggering tasks facing countries that need to feed and educate hungry masses, build a nation, and develop an economy and a society from near zero; but they cannot accept that these require the repudiation of the individual. Legitimate claims of cultural pluralism and of some measure of ethical relativism must not be allowed to dilute essential values and reduce them to matters of opinion or taste. Cultural differences and traditions may explain, even justify, different ways of giving expression to the values accepted by all in the international human rights documents; they cannot explain or justify barbarism and repression. No civilized culture—Eastern or Western, old or new—justifies torture or detention, unfair trials and other injustice, and broad denials of civil rights and liberties or even of political freedoms. Respect for the individual is not a Western monopoly, and, moreover, it did not come naturally to the West. It had to be nurtured there; it has equally fertile soil elsewhere and can be nurtured there.

We are entitled to pursue in our dialogue also, and in particular, the relation of political-civil rights to economic-social welfare. Most states of the world are now committed to an ideology of economic and social development, and that should command our sympathy and support. But the justification of development is the good of individual men and women—not only growth in industrialization and gross national product, but also economic and social benefits and rights for all individuals, now and soon. Must the commitment to development entail abandonment, or postponement, or

diversion, of other essential rights? Are there not different paths
to, and strategies of, development with different implications
and consequences for human rights? It is necessary to explore
together rampant myths and assumptions—that human rights
are a Western luxury, a luxury that the West would impose on
the Third World to frustrate its economic development; that
"poor peoples" do not care about freedom, political participation, civil rights and liberties, or cannot afford them; that
respect for civil-political rights interferes with development
and that new states must choose or at least establish priorities
between them; that development requires "strong government" and that strong government means repressive government; that national commitment to development is "the moral
equivalent of war" and, like war, requires and justifies the
sacrifice of individualism, individual life, liberty, privacy, and
property not only for the duration of a brief emergency, but
indefinitely; that to achieve "basic human needs" one must
sacrifice other human rights. Surely we cannot accept that
development requires or justifies systematic disregard of all of
the various rights that are packaged as political and civil
rights.[54] Perhaps some new societies need time to develop the
institutions and practices by which theoretical popular
sovereignty is translated into effective self-government. Perhaps, in some circumstances, economic development requires
some control, even some "regimentation," for some brief time.
But how many hungry are fed, how much industry is built, by
massacre, torture, and detention, by unfair trials and other
injustices, by abuse of minorities, by denials of freedoms of
conscience, by suppression of political association and
expression? At the behest of the Third World, the UN General
Assembly has declared itself "profoundly convinced that all
human rights and fundamental freedoms are interrelated and
indivisible."[55] To the Third World, that may imply that civil
and political rights cannot flourish where economic-social
rights lag. But it implies equally the reverse, that economic-

social rights can be achieved (and will command domestic and external support) only if basic political-civil rights are respected.

To us, the heirs of an eighteenth-century libertarian tradition, its truths are self-evident. Because of their "natural" appeal, and the fortunes of history, those truths were enshrined after World War II in many national constitutions, in the Universal Declaration of Human Rights, and consequently in international covenants. As a result, our way and our values are the norms and the ideals to which all pay obeisance. But, in fact, these truths are less evident to others, and to some, other models may have stronger appeal. Universal acceptance of our ideas and even of our words is a dangerous compliment, for it threatens that others, not of our persuasion, will seek to distort them to other meanings and other ends. We will have to be alert to attempts to exploit the inevitable inadequacy of words, to extend their peripheral ambiguities in order to erode the hard core of certainty; or to stretch exceptions (e.g., the needs of "national security") until they swallow the stated right. In parts of the Third World, for example, "the Chinese way" has aroused admiration and invited emulation, and the world may yet be offered a new "universal declaration," which would be "collectivist" rather than "individualist," which would subordinate individual freedom, privacy, integrity, dignity, and even equality and justice to the good of the group today or in the future, to alleged requirements of authority, order, and stability to support obvious basic needs or economic development or "nation building."

That human rights are now international business need not confuse us as to our own values, nor does it require us to allow others to distort them. The human rights movement has achieved universal commitment to individual human rights and needs now, not merely to the good of some abstract collectivity someday. Occasional tensions between individual rights and public good, or between competing rights, may require accommodation between them, but that too has to be achieved within the human rights ideology, with respect for the individual welfare, autonomy, and dignity of men and women today and tomorrow.

FOUR

༼ ༽

HOMAGE TO MR. PAINE

In the last quarter of this century, we are celebrating two hundred years of an idea. How much difference have these centuries made? Surely none of us can be happy with the condition of human rights today, but we are not as unhappy, I think, as we might have been—or ought to have been—200 years ago. Even today, the condition of human rights could be much worse. Human rights are philosophically respectable and rhetorically irresistible. Constitutions are de rigueur, and each constitution holds at least the promise and the seed of constitutionalism. The deterrent effect of the international human rights movement, of transnational example and influence, cannot be measured, but neither can it be dismissed: dramatic violations, we know, are deterred or modified, and if transnational scrutiny were not significant, it would not be so strenuously resisted.[1]

Speaking of Magna Carta, of its limited beginnings and its luxuriant growth, Sir Hersch Lauterpacht, one of the godfathers of international human rights, said: "The vindication of human liberties does not begin with their complete and triumphant assertion at the very outset. It commences with their recognition in *some* matters, to *some* extent, for *some* people, against *some* organ of the State."[2] The vindication of the rights of man began 200 years ago, in some matters, to some extent, for some people. Today, human rights are alive, if not wholly well everywhere; but for most people, perhaps everywhere, human rights are much better than they were 200 years ago.

Whether they will be better 200 years from now depends on political and social forces, domestic and international, some now being formed, some not yet conceived or conceivable. Extrapolating from what has happened in 200 years past is risky, for the rate and direction of change might be radically different. But the ideas are here, and if mankind survives, if societies and governments survive, the individual will survive, and his rights will be recognizable to us. Both national and international law will include human rights, both political-civil and economic-social. I cannot accept that what we believe in and do now will be wholly irrelevant in 200 years; surely, they are relevant to how individual men and women will fare ten, twenty, fifty years from now.

Having appropriated the title of Thomas Paine's famous book and invoked him repeatedly, I owe him, perhaps, a final word. Scorned, persecuted, and rejected in his day, he surely deserves better in our day. So many of the issues of our time were addressed by Paine—colonialism and self-determination, the values and the costs of stability and of revolution, the essentials of individual liberty and of democratic government, the welfare state, international peace, even (as someone put it) how people can make sense of their lives without the consolations of revealed religion. Answers that engage and divide students and practitioners of politics today were first impressed on the world by Thomas Paine, and he still speaks to us relevantly and cogently about them. He was a democrat and libertarian, meliorist, and even something of a socialist (small *s*, before the word was common and acquired Marxist connotations). The Englishman who condemned his own government and participated in revolution in two other countries would not have assumed that all is for the best in any one country, that any one political system has a monopoly on virtue and on wisdom. The champion of, the participant in, the

American and the French revolutions, the Quaker who became
a revolutionary, the revolutionary who remained a Quaker,
would note with pleasure what has been achieved and note
with dismay the so-much-that-is-still-to-be-done.

Paine did not father the ideas reflected in the rights of man
today, but he did much to spread and root them, and he
provided us a theology and a terminology, guiding principles
as well as particular blueprints. Being human, he would
doubtless note with deep satisfaction his decisive victory over
Edmund Burke;[3] hereditary monarchy is now a historic fossil.
He who was hounded and persecuted by his own country and
threatened with execution by his beloved French Revolution
would bow to the tribute of 150 states (including his own and
France) representing nearly 4 billion people—all the people of
the world—intoning his words. His prayer in presenting his
book to George Washington, that "the Rights of Man may
become universal," has in one important sense been realized.

Thomas Paine had proclaimed constitutionalism as *the*
right of man and as the foundation of all rights of man: today
constitutionalism is accepted by virtually all, at least in
principle. Paine argued hotly the sovereignty of the people;
today popular sovereignty is accepted almost everywhere, at
least in principle. For Paine, "representative government is
freedom"; today suffrage is universal, and government is
representative everywhere, at least in principle. For Paine,
man's rights were natural, inherent in the equality of God's
human creations, and retained by them pursuant to their social
contract. Today human rights—whether natural, contractual,
psychological, or political as positive law—are accepted by all,
at least in principle.

Paine would be delighted that the purpose of government
has expanded, that government's responsibility for the
economic and social welfare of all the people is now axiomatic;
that his program for social security financed by progressive
taxation is taken for granted in Europe and America; that the
tenets, libertarian as well as socialist, of the French Revolution

and the French Declaration, revolutionary then, are common-place now, at least in constitutional principle. Paine would glow at the realization that self-determination (our word for his idea) is a prominent principle of our times, that international institutions, reflecting universal commitment, try to keep peace between nations (another of his interests) and promote other common goals and ideas—all of them Rights of Man.[4]

If he were to look around the new world today, Thomas Paine would find much to cheer him, but also much to depress him. He would not be unhappy about Great Britain, as he was 200 years ago; he might be less excited about, but still rather pleased with, the United States and France. The proclaimed socialism and egalitarianism of communism, and of other contemporary revolutions, would appeal to him; but he would be horrified, I think, by their essentially unrepresentative government; by dictatorship—even of the proletariat, surely of party; by new, current-style monarchies and monarchs. He would welcome the many new states—the products of revolution and self-determination—and would applaud their devotion in principle to equality, and to individual welfare as of right, not of charity. But he would rage at the suggestion that welfare and equality can be achieved only under autocracy, at the cost of liberty, at the sacrifice of the present for an uncertain future and of living men and women for distant and hypothetical generations to come.

Paine could not help but be pleased that in principle, constitutionalism, popular sovereignty, representative govern-ment, and inherent or retained rights are today established, commonplace, even axiomatic, but he would note soberly, even somberly, that these principles are not realized in too many places, in too many respects. Constitutions often only describe what governments in fact are and do; they do not prescribe what good governments should be, or do, and limit them accordingly. Popular sovereignty is sometimes proclaimed loudest by governments that abuse the people's mandate, disregard their wishes, and violate their interests. Representative government is not freedom when it is honored only in empty forms, sometimes even by compelling the people to signify approval for what and whom they abhor. The rights of men and women are still sometimes only crumbs thrown them by grace of rules; sometimes even these rights are only duties, the "right" to serve.

In a word, Thomas Paine might see the acceptance of his ideas in principle as sometimes hypocritical, as but the homage that vice pays to virtue. But he would not necessarily depreciate even such hypocrisy, for it reflects recognition that human rights are widely considered a good—valued, respected, cared for. With the principle firm and ineradicable, it is less difficult to begin the struggle to make constitutions more meaningful. That the interest of the people is the accepted touchstone of legitimate government gives hope—even, perhaps, renders it likely—that in time more governments will be more representative, and more governments will do better by the people's rights and interests.

Paine proclaimed the rights of man in national society. An apostle of international cooperation, he would have welcomed international human rights, reflecting responsibility beyond and above the nation-state. The first decades of such efforts have brought some successes: perhaps, above all, they have established that how any government behaves is no longer no one else's business. From there, there is a long way to go, and many nations will want—yet resist—transnational influence to show them the way, and to induce them to take it. Will, say, Eleanor Roosevelt, midwife to international human rights, be as content at her bicentennial as Thomas Paine might be today?

In 1790, Thomas Paine wrote George Washington: "I have not the least doubt of the final and complete success of the French Revolution."[5] Today, having seen what two hundred years have wrought—as well as what they have not yet achieved—he might look ahead to the next two hundred years of the rights of man, if not without "the least doubt," at least with hope, perhaps even with confidence.

APPENDIX

᙮

UNIVERSAL DECLARATION OF HUMAN RIGHTS

WHEREAS recognition of the inherent dignity and of the equal and inalienable rights of all members of the human family is the foundation of freedom, justice and peace in the world,

WHEREAS disregard and contempt for human rights have resulted in barbarous acts which have outraged the conscience of mankind, and the advent of a world in which human beings shall enjoy freedom of speech and belief and freedom from fear and want has been proclaimed as the highest aspiration of the common people,

WHEREAS, it is essential, if man is not to be compelled to have recourse, as a last resort, to rebellion against tyranny and oppression, that human rights should be protected by the rule of law,

WHEREAS it is essential to promote the development of friendly relations between nations,

WHEREAS the peoples of the United Nations have in their Charter reaffirmed their faith in fundamental human rights, in the dignity and worth of the human person and in the equal rights of men and women and have determined to promote social progress and better standards of life in larger freedom,

139

WHEREAS Member States have pledged themselves to achieve, in co-operation with the United Nations, the promotion of universal respect for and observance of human rights and fundamental freedoms,

WHEREAS a common understanding of these rights and freedoms is of the greatest importance for the full realization of this pledge,

NOW, THEREFORE, THE GENERAL ASSEMBLY PROCLAIMS this Universal Declaration of Human Rights as a common standard of achievement for all peoples and all nations, to the end that every individual and every organ of society, keeping this Declaration constantly in mind, shall strive by teaching and education to promote respect for these rights and freedoms and by progressive measures, national and international, to secure their universal and effective recognition and observance, both among the peoples of Member States themselves and among the peoples of territories under their jurisdiction.

Article 1. All human beings are born free and equal in dignity and rights. They are endowed with reason and conscience and should act towards one another in a spirit of brotherhood.

Article 2. Everyone is entitled to all the rights and freedoms set forth in this Declaration, without distinction of any kind, such as race, colour, sex, language, religion, political or other opinion, national or social origin, property, birth or other status. Furthermore, no distinction shall be made on the basis of the political, jurisdictional or international status of the country or territory to which a person belongs, whether it be independent, trust, non-self-governing or under any other limitation of sovereignty.

Article 3. Everyone has the right to life, liberty and security of person.

Article 4. No one shall be held in slavery or servitude; slavery and the slave trade shall be prohibited in all their forms.

Article 5. No one shall be subjected to torture or to cruel, inhuman or degrading treatment or punishment.

Article 6. Everyone has the right to recognition everywhere as a person before the law.

Article 7. All are equal before the law and are entitled without discrimination to equal protection of the law. All are entitled to equal protection against any discrimination in violation of this Declaration and against any incitement to such discrimination.

Article 8. Everyone has the right to an effective remedy by the competent national tribunals for acts violating the fundamental rights granted him by the constitution or by law.

Article 9. No one shall be subjected to arbitrary arrest, detention or exile.

Article 10. Everyone is entitled in full equality to a fair and public hearing by an independent and impartial tribunal, in the determination of his rights and obligations and of any criminal charge against him.

Article 11. (1) Everyone charged with a penal offence has the right to be presumed innocent until proved guilty according to law in a public trial at which he has had all the guarantees necessary for his defence.
(2) No one shall be held guilty of any penal offence on account of any act or omission which did not constitute a penal offence, under national or international law, at the time when it was committed. Nor shall a heavier penalty be imposed than the

one that was applicable at the time the penal offence was committed.

Article 12. No one shall be subjected to arbitrary interference with his privacy, family, home or correspondence, nor to attacks upon his honour and reputation. Everyone has the right to the protection of the law against such interference or attacks.

Article 13. (1) Everyone has the right to freedom of movement and residence within the borders of each state.
(2) Everyone has the right to leave any country, including his own, and to return to his country.

Article 14. (1) Everyone has the right to seek and to enjoy in other countries asylum from persecution.
(2) This right may not be invoked in the case of prosecutions genuinely arising from non-political crimes or from acts contrary to the purposes and principles of the United Nations.

Article 15. (1) Everyone has the right to a nationality.
(2) No one shall be arbitrarily deprived of his nationality nor denied the right to change his nationality.

Article 16. (1) Men and women of full age, without any limitation due to race, nationality or religion, have the right to marry and to found a family. They are entitled to equal rights as to marriage, during marriage and at its dissolution.
(2) Marriage shall be entered into only with the free and full consent of the intending spouses.
(3) The family is the natural and fundamental group unit of society and is entitled to protection by society and the State.

Article 17. (1) Everyone has the right to own property alone as well as in association with others.
(2) No one shall be arbitrarily deprived of his property.

Article 18. Everyone has the right to freedom of thought, conscience and religion; this right includes freedom to change his religion or belief, and freedom, either alone or in community with others and in public or private, to manifest his religion or belief in teaching, practice, worship and observance.

Article 19. Everyone has the right to freedom of opinion and expression; this right includes freedom to hold opinions without interference and to seek, receive and impart information and ideas through any media and regardless of frontiers.

Article 20. (1) Everyone has the right to freedom of peaceful assembly and association.
(2) No one may be compelled to belong to an association.

Article 21. (1) Everyone has the right to take part in the government of his country, directly or through freely chosen representatives.
(2) Everyone has the right of equal access to public service in his country.
(3) The will of the people shall be the basis of the authority of government; this will shall be expressed in periodic and genuine elections which shall be by universal and equal suffrage and shall be held by secret vote or by equivalent free voting procedures.

Article 22. Everyone, as a member of society, has the right to social security and is entitled to realization, through national effort and international cooperation and in accordance with the organization and resources of each State, of the economic, social and cultural rights indispensable for his dignity and the free development of his personality.

Article 23. (1) Everyone has the right to work, to free choice of employment, to just and favourable conditions of work and to protection against unemployment.

(2) Everyone, without any discrimination, has the right to equal pay for equal work.

(3) Everyone who works has the right to just and favourable remuneration ensuring for himself and his family an existence worthy of human dignity, and supplemented, if necessary, by other means of social protection.

(4) Everyone has the right to form and to join trade unions for the protection of his interests.

Article 24. Everyone has the right to rest and leisure, including reasonable limitation of working hours and periodic holidays with pay.

Article 25. (1) Everyone has the right to a standard of living adequate for the health and well-being of himself and of his family, including food, clothing, housing and medical care and necessary social services, and the right to security in the event of unemployment, sickness, disability, widowhood, old age or other lack of livelihood in circumstances beyond his control.

(2) Motherhood and childhood are entitled to special care and assistance. All children, whether born in or out of wedlock, shall enjoy the same social protection.

Article 26. (1) Everyone has the right to education. Education shall be free, at least in the elementary and fundamental stages. Elementary education shall be compulsory. Technical and professional education shall be made generally available and higher eduction shall be equally accessible to all on the basis of merit.

(2) Education shall be directed to the full development of the human personality and to the strengthening of respect for human rights and fundamental freedoms. It shall promote understanding, tolerance and friendship among all nations, racial or religious groups, and shall further the activities of the United Nations for the maintenance of peace.

(3) Parents have a prior right to choose the kind of education that shall be given to their children.

Article 27. (1) Everyone has the right freely to participate in the cultural life of the community, to enjoy the arts and to share in scientific advancement and its benefits.
(2) Everyone has the right to the protection of the moral and material interests resulting from any scientific, literary or artistic production of which he is the author.

Article 28. Everyone is entitled to a social and international order in which the rights and freedoms set forth in this Declaration can be fully realized.

Article 29. (1) Everyone has duties to the community in which alone the free and full development of his personality is possible.
(2) In the exercise of his rights and freedoms, everyone shall be subject only to such limitations as are determined by law solely for the purpose of securing due recognition and respect for the rights and freedoms of others and of meeting the just requirements of morality, public order and the general welfare in a democratic society.
(3) These rights and freedoms may in no case be exercised contrary to the purposes and principles of the United Nations.

Article 30. Nothing in this Declaration may be interpreted as implying for any State, group or person any right to engage in any activity or to perform any act aimed at the destruction of any of the rights and freedoms set forth herein.

NOTES

Introduction

1. The American Declaration and the American Revolution, in turn, owed debts to Thomas Paine's powerful and prophetic *Common Sense* of 1775. Of course, they had earlier philosophical foundations. See pp.4-5 above. References to Paine's *The Rights of Man* in these notes are to the Pelican Classic edition, Henry Collins, ed. (1969) (hereinafter cited as Paine).

2. I have noted that the authentic descendants of the Declaration were the early state constitutions; the U.S. Constitution, deriving from the Articles of Confederation and its concerns with union, was only a collateral heir. Chapter 2, pp. 35-36. See Henkin, "Constitutional Fathers, Constitutional Sons," 60 *Minn. L. Rev.* 1113 (1976).

3. Scott v. Sandford, 60 U.S. (19 How.) 393 (1857), held, inter alia, that for Congress to purport to free the slave deprived his master of property without due process of law, in violation of the Fifth Amendment.

4. Nevertheless, Lord Acton thought the Declaration defective, and its defects "a peril and a snare." *Lectures on the French Revolution* (Figgis and Laurence eds. 1910) 107.

5. Bentham, "Anarchical Fallacies," 2 *Works of Jeremy Bentham* 489, 501 (John Bowring ed. 1843).

6. For wide-ranging collections of philosophical essays, see UNESCO, *Human Rights: Comments and Interpretations* (1949); *Le Fondement des Droits de L'Homme*, Actes des Entretiens de L'Aquila, Institut International de Philosophie 1964 (1966); *The Monist*, vol. 52 no. 4 (October 1968); *Human Rights* (A. I. Melden ed. 1970); *Human Rights* (E. H. Pollack ed.), Amintaphil I, papers

prepared for the Secondary Plenary Meeting of the American Section of the International Association for the Philosophy of Law and Social Philosophy 1971. See also *Political Theory and the Rights of Man* (D. D. Raphael ed. 1967); M. Cranston, *What Are Human Rights?* (1973). Compare Claude, "The Classical Model of Human Rights Development," in *Comparative Human Rights* (R. P. Claude ed. 1976), Chapter 1.

Chapter 1

1. Sierra Club v. Morton, 405 U.S. 727, 745 (1972).

2. See Henkin, "Judaism and Human Rights," *Judaism,* Fall 1976.

3. 1 Samuel 8:6-7.

4. Deuteronomy 12:8; Judges 17:6.

5. Genesis 18:24-25; Leviticus 19:15; Deuteronomy 16:20.

6. Genesis 1:26-27, 2:7; Malachi 2:10.

7. Exodus 1:15-17; 1 Samuel 22:17; Daniel 6:10.

8. See, generally, Passerin d'Entreves, *The Case For Natural Law Re-Examined* (1956); and idem, *Natural Law* (1965).

9. D'Entreves, *The Case for Natural Law Re-Examined,* pp. 30-33; idem, *Natural Law,* Chapter 1.

10. See pp. 21-23.

11. From the Declaration of Independence. The original capitalization has been modernized here and in other eighteenth-century documents quoted.

12. Paine 88.

13. Paine 90.

14. Loan Association v. Topeka, 87 U.S. (20 Wall.) 655, 663 (1875).

15. Paine 91.

16. The "social compact," implied in the Virginia Declaration (p. 6), is explicit in the Massachusetts constitution of 1780.

17. U.S. Constitution, Preamble. On the significance of a "constitution," see Chapter 2, pp. 31-32.

18. Paine 63-64.

19. See, generally, Ebinghaus, "Le Système Kantien des Droits de L'Homme et du Citoyen dans sa Signification Historique et Actuelle," and Lowith, "Human Rights in Rousseau, Hegel, and Marx," in *Le Fondement des Droits de L'Homme* (Introduction, note 6), pp. 49, 58.

20. See J. Sullivan, "The Antecedents of the Declaration of Independence," in *Report of the American Historical Association* (1902), vol. 1, p. 67.

21. See, e.g., Kotarbinski, "Les Postulats de la Liberté In-dividuelle," in *Le Fondement des Droits de L'Homme*, p. 36.

22. Griswold, *The Fifth Amendment Today* (1955) 31. Compare Jurow, "Untimely Thoughts: A Reconsideration of the Origins of Due Process of Law," 19 *Am. J. Legal Hist.* 265 (1975).

23. Paine 223. James Madison equated representative government with "republic." *The Federalist* no. 10; cf. no. 39.

24. *The Federalist* no. 47 (Madison).

25. "The doctrine of the separation of powers was adopted by the Convention of 1787, not to promote efficiency but to preclude the exercise of arbitrary power. The purpose was, not to avoid friction, but by means of the inevitable friction incident to the distribution of the governmental powers among three departments, to save the people from autocracy." Justice Brandeis dissenting in Myers v. United States, 272 U.S. 52, 293 (1926). The French Declaration, too, asserts that "A society in which the guarantee of rights is not assured or the separation of powers is not determined has no constitution at all" (Article 16).

26. "In a single republic, all the power surrendered by the people is submitted to the administration of a single government; and the usurpations are guarded against by a division of the government into distinct and separate departments. In the compound republic of America, the power surrendered by the people is first divided between two distinct governments, and then the portion allotted to each subdivided among distinct and separate departments. Hence a double security arises to the rights of the people. The different governments will control each other, at the same time that each will be controlled by itself." *The Federalist* no. 51 (Madison). Cf.: "Time has not lessened the concern of the Founders in devising a federal system which would likewise be a safeguard against arbitrary government." Frankfurter, J., in Bartkus v. Illinois, 359 U.S. 121, 137 (1959); also San Diego Building Trades Council v. Garmon, 359 U.S. 236, 243 (1959) ("the principle of diffusion of power not as a matter of doctrinaire localism but as promoter of democracy"). See Henkin, "Voice of a Modern Federalism," in *Felix Frankfurter: The Judge* (W. Mendelson ed. 1964) 68, 70-73.

Lord Acton saw federalism as the only way to reconcile liberty and democracy; it was a check on democracy, on the majority as on the whole people, and provided "essential security for freedom in every genuine democracy." See Lord Acton, *Lectures on the French Revolution* (Figgis and Laurence eds. 1910) 37, also 20; idem, "Sir Erskine May's Democracy in Europe," in *History of Freedom and Other Essays* (Figgis and Laurence eds. 1922) 98. Lord Acton may have been including in "federalism" not only division of authority between state and nation but also separation of powers, limitations on government, an independent judiciary, and judicial review.

27. Loan Association v. Topeka, 87 U.S. (20 Wall.) 655, 662 (1875).

28. *The Federalist* no. 84 (Hamilton). See Henkin, Introduction, note 2. The original constitution barred ex post facto laws and bills of attainder, by both federal and state governments, and forbade the states to impair contracts. It also limited the power to suspend the privilege of habeas corpus, prescribed local, jury trial in federal criminal cases, and established procedures and penalties in trials for treason and in impeachment proceedings. The desire to secure out-of-state citizens against prejudice was one of the purposes of establishing the federal judiciary and the clause in Article IV requiring states to respect the privileges and immunities of citizens of other states.

29. U.S. Constitution, Preamble, and Article I, Section 8, clause 1. One hundred fifty years later, the power of Congress to tax and spend for the general welfare became the principal vehicle for making us a welfare state. See Chapter 2, p. 49.

30. See, e.g., New Hampshire, constitution of 1792, Article VI; Vermont, constitution of 1793, sec. 41; Maine, constitution of 1819, Article VIII.

31. Only the privilege of the writ of habeas corpus may be suspended. Article I, Section 9. See Chapter 2, p. 38. As regards the duties of individuals, cf. the constitutions of the USSR and China (Chapter 2); also the Universal Declaration, Article 29(1); and the preamble to the International Covenant on Civil and Political Rights.

32. Article IX. In 1895, the Supreme Court held that the presumption of innocence was part of the common law of evidence; it cited no constitutional provisions and did not suggest that it is constitutionally required. Coffin v. United States, 156 U.S. 432 (1895); cf. Stack v. Boyle, 342 U.S. 1, 4 (1951). Today the presumption of innocence is implied in the constitutional requirement that the state prove its case against one accused of crime beyond a reasonable doubt. In re *Winship*, 397 U.S. 358 (1970); cf. Leland v. Oregon, 343 U.S. 790 (1952).

The French Declaration also articulated, as the U.S. Bill of Rights does not, limitations on rights, e.g., that "every citizen may speak, write and publish freely, but he is responsible for the abuse of this liberty in cases determined by the law" (Article XI). Limitations are in fact read into the Bill of Rights. See Chapter 2, p. 47-48.

33. Articles IV, V, VI, XIII. Paine was also an early exponent of progressive taxation, as of universal suffrage. Paine 246 et seq.

34. Compare R. Sokol, *Justice after Darwin* (1975), Chapter 5.

35. See Chapter 2, pp. 42-43.

36. Ibid.

37. The phrase is Jerome Frank's. Frank, "Interpretations of Modern Legal Philosophies," *Essays in Honor of Roscoe Pound* (1947) 223.

38. Paine 136.

39. Bentham, "Anarchical Fallacies," p. 502.

40. Herbert Spencer invoked natural law against "meddling legislation" and taxation for social purposes. See H. Lauterpacht, *International Law and Human Rights* (1973) 76. Compare Bentham, "Anarchical Fallacies," p. 105n.

41. J. Austin, *The Province of Jurisprudence Determined* (1861) 118.

42. "In the opinion of Marxism, the liberation of the individual is impossible until the mass has been liberated." J. Stalin, "Anarchism or Socialism," 1 *Sochineniia* [Collected works] (1946) 295-296, quoted in *The Soviet Legal System* (Hazard, Butler, and Maggs eds., 3d ed. 1977) 84. Compare Marx, quoted Chapter 2, note 74.

43. See Chapter 2, pp. 57-60.

44. Compare Chapter 2, pp. 57 et seq.; also Chapter 3, pp. 98-99, 111, 129-31.

45. Chapter 3, pp. 111, 129-31.

46. See Chapter 2.

47. "Certainly there was, just a relatively few years ago, fairly general agreement that the doctrine of natural rights had been thoroughly and irretrievably discredited. Indeed, this was sometimes looked upon as the paradigm case of the manner in which a moral and political doctrine could be both rhetorically influential and intellectually inadequate and unacceptable." R. Wasserstrom, "Rights, Human Rights, and Racial Discrimination," 61 *Journal of Philosophy* no. 20 (1964), reprinted in *Human Rights* (Melden ed. 1970) 96.

48. U.S. Constitution, Article VI, Section 2.

49. Marbury v. Madison, 5 U.S. (1 Cranch) 137 (1803); Fletcher v. Peck, 10 U.S. (6 Cranch) 87 (1810).

50. See Fletcher v. Peck, 10 U.S. (6 Cranch) 87, 135 (1810). Cf. Calder v. Bull, 3 U.S. (3 Dall.) 386 (1798); Loan Association v. Topeka, 87 U.S. (20 Wall.) 655, 663 (1875). Marshall, I have noted, laid the early blocks of judicial review without flouting powerful political forces. See Henkin, "Constitutional Fathers," pp. 1140-1141.

51. E.g., United States v. Nixon, 418 U.S. 683 (1974); Youngstown

Sheet & Tube Co. v. Sawyer, 343 U.S. 579 (1952).

52. See Cooper v. Aaron, 358 U.S. 1 (1958); President Franklin Roosevelt's "Gold Clause" speech, 1 *F.D.R.: His Personal Letters, 1928-45* (Elliot Roosevelt ed. 1957).

53. Compare the extended controversy between Justice Frankfurter and Justice Black. Adamson v. California, 332 U.S. 46, at 59 and 68 (1947).

54. Griswold v. Connecticut, 381 U.S. 479 (1965); Roe v. Wade, 410 U.S. 113 (1973). See Henkin, "Privacy and Autonomy," 74 *Colum. L. Rev.* 1410 (1974).

55. See Chapter 3.

56. Although in some countries domestic courts will apply domestic law even if it is inconsistent with an international norm or obligation, that puts the state in default on its international undertaking. For the law in the United States, see Henkin, *Foreign Affairs and the Constitution* (1972) 163-164, 221-222; but cf. Article 55 of the French constitution of 1958 and Articles 65-66 of the constitution of the Netherlands.

57. Compare Henkin, *How Nations Behave* (1968), Chapter 2.

58. Among the early antecedents of international law was the *ius gentium* of Ancient Rome, which virtually became identified with *ius naturale* ("natural law"). See generally H. Lauterpacht, *International Law and Human Rights* (1973), pt. 1, sect. 2. See Chapter 3, note 1 below.

59. See Chapter 3.

60. Cranston, *What Are Human Rights?* p. 65. He said also: "I believe that a philosophically respectable concept of human rights has been muddled, obscured and debilitated in recent years by attempts to incorporate into it specific rights of a different logical category."

61. Compare President Franklin Roosevelt's economic bill of rights in his State of the Union Message, January 11, 1944, 90 *Cong. Rec.* 78th Cong., 2d sess., pp. 55-57. Congress passed something essentially different from the "full employment" bill proposed in 1945. Compare 90 *Cong. Rec.* 9759 with 60 *Stat.* 23 (1946).

62. Acton, *History of Freedom and Other Essays*, p. 88.

63. U.S. Constitution, Amendment XIV. See Chapter 2.

64. See Chapter 2.

65. Chapter 2, pp. 59-60.

66. See Chapter 3.

67. Jefferson, *Democracy* (S. K. Padover ed. 1939) 76-77.

Chapter 2

1. See, generally, C. H. McIlwain, *Constitutionalism Ancient and Modern* (1940), especially Chapters 1 and 2.

2. The constitutions of the countries of the world are compiled in Blaustein and Flanz, *Constitutions of the Countries of the World* (1971–); also Peaslee, *Constitutions of Nations* (rev. 3d ed. 1970, rev. 4th ed. 1974).

3. Canadian Bill of Rights Act, S.C. 1960, 8-9 Elizabeth II c. 44. And see note 80 below.

4. In the United States, for example, unless the Constitution were abrogated or amended, even a national referendum could not impose segregation. Compare Reitman v. Mulkey, 387 U.S. 369 (1967) (state referendum); Lucas v. Forty-fourth General Assembly, 377 U.S. 713 (1964). Compare Lord Acton, who found the American Constitution admirable because it set up safeguards against "the power of its own sovereign people," because unlike other democracies the United States respected "freedom, authority, and law." *History of Freedom and Other Essays* (Figgis and Laurence eds. 1922) 85. Compare Chapter 1, pp. 10-11.

5. Compare Chapter 1, p. 11; Henkin, "Constitutional Fathers, Constitutional Sons," 60 *Minn. L. Rev.* 1113 (1976).

6. Ibid.

7. Harper v. Virginia State Board of Elections, 383 U.S. 663 (1966) (state elections).

8. The privilege of the writ was suspended by President Lincoln during the Civil War; in a few counties in South Carolina after the Civil War (to combat the Ku Klux Klan); in the Philippines in 1905; in Hawaii during World War II. See *The Constitution of the United States of America: Analysis and Interpretation* (Jayson et al., eds. 1973) 365. The power of the president to suspend the writ on his own authority was challenged by Chief Justice Taney in *Ex parte* Merryman, 17 Fed. Cas. 144 (no. 9487) (C.C.D. Md. 1861); compare *Ex parte* Milligan, 71 U.S. (4 Wall.) 2 (1866).

The relocation of Americans during World War II was upheld in Korematsu v. United States, 323 U.S. 214 (1944); cf. Hirabayashi v. United States, 320 U.S. 81 (1943); but cf. *Ex parte* Endo, 323 U.S. 283 (1944). The constitutional claims of alien enemies relocated and detained during the war were rejected in Ludecke v. Watkins, 335 U.S. 160 (1948). Some may see major derogations from rights in the prosecution of communist leaders for subversive activities, prosecution upheld by the Supreme Court. Dennis v. United States, 341 U.S. 494 (1951). But that case has now been substantially limited. Yates v. United States, 354 U.S. 298 (1957); Scales v. United States, 367 U.S. 203 (1961); Noto v. United States, 367 U.S. 290 (1961). The subversive activities legislation has been virtually a dead letter, and its repeal is expected.

9. United States v. United States District Court, 407 U.S. 297 (1972); Zweibon v. Mitchell, 516 F. 2d 594 (D.C. Cir. 1975), *cert. denied,* 425 U.S. 944 (1976). Compare Youngstown Sheet & Tube Co. v. Sawyer, 343 U.S. 579 (1952) (requiring the president to return private property held improperly seized).

10. For recent "rectifications," cf. the Case Act, 86 *Stat.* 619, 1 U.S.C. sec. 112b (1976) (requiring the president to report on executive agreements); the War Powers Resolution, 87 *Stat.* 555, 50 U.S.C. sec. 1541 (Supp. V, 1975); the Congressional Budget and Impoundment Control Act, 88 *Stat.* 297, 31 U.S.C. sec. 1301 (Supp. V, 1975).

11. Buckley v. Valeo, 424 U.S. 1 (1976).

12. Compare Justice Brandeis, quoted Chapter 1, note 25.

13. See Henkin, "Some Reflections on Current Constitutional Controversy," 109 *U. Pa. L. Rev.* 637, 645 (1961); also Henkin, "Constitutional Fathers," p. 1128.

14. National League of Cities v. Usery, 426 U.S. 833 (1976).

15. See Chapter 1, note 26.

16. Harper v. Virginia State Board of Elections, 383 U.S. 663 (1966); see U.S. Constitution, Amendment XXIV. Requiring literacy was held constitutionally permissible, Lassiter v. Northampton Board of Election, 360 U.S. 45 (1959), but it was outlawed by Congress in the Voting Rights Act of 1965, 79 *Stat.* 437, sec. 4, 42 U.S.C. sec. 1973 (1970). See Katzenbach v. Morgan, 384 U.S. 641 (1966); also South Carolina v. Katzenbach, 383 U.S. 301 (1966). Extended residence requirements for voting have been held to violate the right to travel. Dunn v. Blumstein, 405 U.S. 330 (1972). But a state may continue to deny the right to vote to those convicted of felony. Richardson v. Ramirez, 418 U.S. 24 (1974).

17. Baker v. Carr, 369 U.S. 186 (1962); Reynolds v. Sims, 377 U.S. 533 (1964).

18. See Henkin, "Some Reflections on Current Constitutional Controversy," p. 646. But cf. the *National League of Cities* case, (note 14 above); its significance for federalism and judicial review remains to be seen.

19. Cooper v. Aaron, 358 U.S. 1 (1958); cf. United States v. Nixon, 418 U.S. 683 (1974). Cf. Mr. Justice Jackson: "We are not final

because we are infallible, but we are infallible only because we are final." Brown v. Allen, 344 U.S. 443, 540 (1953) (concurring opinion).

20. I draw here on Henkin, "Constitutional Fathers."

21. Cf. A. Meikeljohn, *Free Speech and Its Relation to Self-Government* (1948), especially Chapter 4; and Z. Chafee's review of that book, 62 *Harv. L. Rev.* 891 (1949). Cf. the Alien and Sedition Laws of 1798; see J. M. Smith, *Freedom's Fetters* (1956). The Alien and Sedition Laws were upheld in the lower courts but expired before the Supreme Court could rule on their constitutional validity.

22. Barron v. Baltimore, 32 U.S. (7 Pet.) 243 (1833).

23. Compare Dartmouth College v. Woodward, 17 U.S. (4 Wheat.) 518 (1819); Fletcher v. Peck, 10 U.S. (6 Cranch) 87 (1810); Sturges v. Crowninshield, 17 U.S. (4 Wheat.) 122 (1819); Green v. Biddle, 21 U.S. (8 Wheat.) 1 (1823).

24. Scott v. Sandford, 60 U.S. (19 How.) 393 (1857). See Introduction, note 3.

25. Afroyim v. Rusk, 387 U.S. 253 (1967); also Schneider v. Rusk, 377 U.S. 163 (1964); but cf. Rogers v. Bellei, 401 U.S. 815 (1971), limiting that doctrine to citizenship at birth or acquired by naturalization, not to citizenship granted by Congress to one born abroad of an American parent.

26. Civil Rights Cases, 109 U.S. 3 (1883); cf. Grovey v. Townsend, 295 U.S. 45 (1935), *overruled,* Smith v. Allwright, 321 U.S. 649 (1944); also Slaughter-House Cases, 83 U.S. (16 Wall.) 36 (1873).

27. Pollock v. Farmers' Loan and Trust Co., 157 U.S. 429 (1895); Hammer v. Dagenhart, 247 U.S. 251 (1918); cf. Bailey v. Drexel Furniture Co., 259 U.S. 20 (1922). Also Schechter Poultry Corp. v. United States, 295 U.S. 495 (1935); Carter v. Carter Coal Co., 298 U.S. 238 (1936).

28. Lochner v. New York, 198 U.S. 45 (1905); Adair v. United States, 208 U.S. 161 (1908); Coppage v. Kansas, 236 U.S. 1 (1915); Adkins v. Children's Hospital, 261 U.S. 525 (1923); Morehead v. New York *ex rel.* Tipaldo, 298 U.S. 587 (1936). All these cases were later overruled. West Coast Hotel Co. v. Parrish, 300 U.S. 379 (1937); United States v. Darby, 312 U.S. 100 (1941); Phelps Dodge Corp. v. NLRB, 313 U.S. 177 (1941); Lincoln Fed. Labor Union v. Northwestern Iron & Met. Co., 335 U.S. 525 (1949).

29. Plessy v. Ferguson, 163 U.S. 537 (1896); Bradwell v. State, 83 U.S. (16 Wall.) 130 (1873). Cf. notes 52 and 53.

30. Schenck v. United States, 249 U.S. 47 (1919); Debs v. United States, 249 U.S. 211 (1919); Abrams v. United States, 250 U.S. 616 (1919); Gitlow v. New York, 268 U.S. 652 (1925); Whitney v. California 274 U.S. 357 (1927).

31. Olmstead v. United States, 277 U.S. 438 (1928), *overruled*, Berger v. New York, 388 U.S. 41 (1967).

32. The cases are collected in Duncan v. Louisiana, 391 U.S. 145, 147-149 (1968). See Henkin, " 'Selective Incorporation' in the Fourteenth Amendment," 73 *Yale L. J.* 74 (1963).

33. Griswold v. Connecticut, 381 U.S. 479 (1965). Later the Court found the right of privacy to be a form of liberty protected by the due process clause. See Roe v. Wade, note 34 below.

34. Griswold v. Connecticut, 381 U.S. 479 (1965) (contraception); Roe v. Wade, 410 U.S. 113 (1973) (abortion); Meyer v. Nebraska, 262 U.S. 390 (1923) (parental education of children); cf. Wisconsin v. Yoder, 406 U.S. 205 (1972); but cf. Doe v. Commonwealth's Attorney, 403 F. Supp. 1199 (E.D. Va. 1975), *affirmed without opinion*, 425 U.S. 901 (1976) (upholding sodomy law); Kelley v. Johnson, 425 U.S. 238 (1976) (policeman's hair length). Cf. Stanley v. Georgia, 394 U.S. 557 (1969) and Paris Adult Theater I v. Slaton, 413 U.S. 49 (1973).

35. Cantwell v. Connecticut, 310 U.S. 296 (1940); Thornhill v. Alabama, 310 U.S. 88 (1940); Virginia State Board of Pharmacy v. Virginia Citizens Consumer Council, Inc., 425 U.S. 748 (1976); Kingsley International Picture Corp. v. Regents, 360 U.S. 684 (1959); Memoirs v. Massachusetts, 383 U.S. 413 (1966); Stanley v. Georgia, 394 U.S. 557 (1969); Cohen v. California, 403 U.S. 15 (1971); Miller v. California, 413 U.S. 15 (1973); Jenkins v. Georgia, 418 U.S. 153 (1974); Erzoznik v. City of Jacksonville, 422 U.S. 205 (1975).

36. Tinker v. Des Moines School District, 393 U.S. 503 (1969); West Virginia State Board of Education v. Barnette, 319 U.S. 624, 632-633 (1943); also Brown v. Louisiana, 383 U.S. 131 (1966); Wooley v. Maynard, 430 U.S. 705 (1977). See Henkin, "The Supreme Court, 1967 Term. Foreword: On Drawing Lines," 82 *Harv. L. Rev.* 63, 76-82 (1968).

37. Buckley v. Valeo, 424 U.S. 1 (1976).

38. New York Times v. United States, 403 U.S. 713 (1971); New York Times v. Sullivan, 376 U.S. 254 (1964); Curtis Publishing Co. v. Butts, 388 U.S. 130 (1967); Time, Inc. v. Hill, 385 U.S. 374 (1967); cf. Cox Broadcasting, Inc. v. Cohen, 420 U.S. 469 (1975). But cf. Gertz v. Robert Welch, Inc., 418 U.S. 323 (1974); Time, Inc. v. Firestone, 424 U.S. 448 (1976).

39. Hague v. CIO, 307 U.S. 496 (1939); Marsh v. Alabama, 326 U.S. 501 (1946); Cox v. Louisiana, 379 U.S. 536 (1965); cf. Red Lion Broadcasting Co. v. FCC, 395 U.S. 367 (1969) and Columbia Broadcasting System v. Democratic National Comm., 412 U.S. 94 (1973); Talley v. California, 362 U.S. 60 (1960); Sweezy v. New

Hampshire, 354 U.S. 234 (1957); Miami Herald Pub. Co. v. Tornillo, 418 U.S. 241 (1974); Baird v. State Bar of Arizona, 401 U.S. 1 (1971). For the long, tortuous history of Supreme Court handling of governmental loyalty oaths and investigations, see Gunther, *Cases and Materials on Constitutional Law* (9th ed. 1975) 1376 et seq.

40. NAACP v. Alabama, 357 U.S. 449 (1958); Shelton v. Tucker, 364 U.S. 479 (1960); Gibson v. Florida Legislative Investigation Comm., 372 U.S. 539 (1963); De Gregory v. New Hampshire Attorney General, 383 U.S. 825 (1966); Baird v. State Bar of Arizona, 401 U.S. 1 (1971).

41. Sherbert v. Verner, 374 U.S. 398 (1963); but cf. Trans World Airlines, Inc. v. Hardison, 432 U.S. 63 (1977).

42. Everson v. Board of Education, 330 U.S. 1 (1947); Lemon v. Kurtzman, 403 U.S. 602 (1971); School District of Abington v. Schempp, 374 U.S. 203 (1963); Engel v. Vitale, 370 U.S. 421 (1962). Compare Tilton v. Richardson, 403 U.S. 672 (1971); Roemer v. Maryland Public Works Board, 426 U.S. 736 (1976).

43. Berger v. New York, 388 U.S. 41 (1967); Katz v. United States, 389 U.S. 347 (1967).

44. Camara v. Municipal Court, 387 U.S. 523 (1967); cf. Wyman v. James, 400 U.S. 309 (1971) (visit by social worker).

45. Mapp v. Ohio, 367 U.S. 643 (1961); Gideon v. Wainwright, 372 U.S. 335 (1963); Malloy v. Hogan, 378 U.S. 1 (1964); cf. Griffin v. California, 380 U.S. 609 (1965).

46. Robinson v. California, 370 U.S. 660 (1962); cf. Powell v. Texas, 392 U.S. 514 (1968). Also Weems v. United States, 217 U.S. 349 (1910); Coker v. Georgia, 433 U.S. 584 (1977); cf. Commonwealth v. O'Neal, note 47 below.

47. Compare the discussion of the purposes of the death penalty in Gregg v. Georgia, 428 U.S. 153 (1976) with the discussion in Commonwealth v. O'Neal, 339 N.E. 2d 676 (Mass. 1975), decided under the "cruel or unusual punishment" clause of the Massachusetts constitution. Cf. also the *Coker* case, note 46 above.

48. Cf. Furman v. Georgia 408 U.S. 238 (1972); Gregg v. Georgia, 428 U.S. 153 (1976); Woodson v. North Carolina, 428 U.S. 280 (1976). Cf. also the various opinions in Commonwealth v. O'Neal, note 47 above.

49. See note 17 above.

50. See, e.g., Bolling v. Sharpe, 347 U.S. 497 (1954); Schneider v. Rusk, 377 U.S. 163 (1964); Schlesinger v. Ballard, 419 U.S. 498, 500 n. 3 (1975); Weinberger v. Wiesenfeld, 420 U.S. 636, 638 n. 2 (1976).

51. Smith v. Texas, 311 U.S. 128, 132 (1940).

52. Brown v. Board of Education, 347 U.S. 483 (1954), *overruling* Plessy v. Ferguson, 163 U.S. 537 (1896), note 29 above; also Bolling v. Sharpe, 347 U.S. 497 (1954).

53. Taylor v. Louisiana, 419 U.S. 522 (1975); Weinberger v. Wiesenfeld, 420 U.S. 636 (1975); Frontiero v. Richardson, 411 U.S. 677 (1973); Reed v. Reed, 404 U.S. 71 (1971). For the earlier view, now rejected, cf. the *Bradwell* case, note 29 above. Also Craig v. Boren, 429 U.S. 190 (1976).

54. Griffin v. Illinois, 351 U.S. 12 (1956); Boddie v. Connecticut, 401 U.S. 371 (1971); but cf. United States v. Kras, 409 U.S. 434 (1973).

55. Graham v. Richardson, 403 U.S. 365 (1971); Sugarman v. Dougall, 413 U.S. 634 (1973); in re Griffiths, 413 U.S. 717 (1973); cf. Hampton v. Mow Sun Wong, 426 U.S. 88 (1976); but cf. Mathews v. Diaz, 426 U.S. 67 (1976). Also Yick Wo v. Hopkins, 118 U.S. 356 (1886); Truax v. Raich, 239 U.S. 33 (1915); Takahashi v. Fish and Game Comm., 334 U.S. 410 (1948).

56. Trimble v. Gordon, 430 U.S. 762 (1977); Jiminez v. Weinberger, 417 U.S. 628 (1974); Weber v. Aetna Casualty & Surety Co., 406 U.S. 164 (1972); Levy v. Louisiana, 391 U.S. 68 (1968); cf. Labine v. Vincent, 401 U.S. 532 (1971); but cf. Mathews v. Lucas, 427 U.S. 495 (1976).

57. Cruz v. Beto, 405 U.S. 319 (1972); Pell v. Procunier, 417 U.S. 817, 822 (1974) (prisoners); O'Connor v. Donaldson, 422 U.S. 563 (1975) (mental patients); Goss v. Lopez, 419 U.S. 565 (1975) (schoolchildren); Planned Parenthood of Central Missouri v. Danforth, 428 U.S. 52 (1976); Carey v. Population Services International, 431 U.S. 678 (1977); cf. Wisconsin v. Yoder, 406 U.S. 205, 241 (1972) (Douglas, J., dissenting in part).

58. Kent v. Dulles, 357 U.S. 116 (1958); Shapiro v. Thompson, 394 U.S. 618 (1969); Oregon v. Mitchell, 400 U.S. 112 (1970); Dunn v. Blumstein, 405 U.S. 330 (1972); Memorial Hospital v. Maricopa County, 415 U.S. 250 (1974). But cf. Sosna v. Iowa, 419 U.S. 393 (1975).

59. Griswold v. Connecticut, 381 U.S. 479 (1965); Roe v. Wade, 410 U.S. 113 (1973); Stanley v. Georgia, 394 U.S. 557 (1969). See Henkin, "Privacy and Autonomy," 74 *Colum. L. Rev.* 1410 (1970). But cf. Doe v. Commonwealth's Attorney, note 34 above (sodomy).

60. Pierce v. Society of Sisters, 268 U.S. 510 (1925); Wisconsin v. Yoder 406 U.S. 205 (1972) (compulsory high school attendance law violates Amish parents' freedom of religion).

61. Cf. Sierra Club v. Morton, Chapter 1, p. 1n.

62. Thompson v. Louisville, 362 U.S. 199 (1960); Papachristou v. City of Jacksonville, 405 U.S. 156 (1972); Palmer v. City of Euclid, 402

U.S. 544 (1971). See Amsterdam, "The Void-for-Vagueness Doctrine in the Supreme Court," 109 *U. Pa. L. Rev.* 67 (1960). Also NAACP v. Button, 371 U.S. 415 (1963); Keyishian v. Board of Regents, 385 U.S. 589 (1967). But cf. Colten v. Kentucky, 407 U.S. 104 (1972) (disorderly conduct); Parker v. Levy, 417 U.S. 733 (1974) (military conviction for "conduct unbecoming an officer").

63. Nebbia v. New York, 291 U.S. 502 (1934). This remains of the substantive due process doctrine, which flourished until 1936, note 28 above. The doctrine has been used to support liberties not elsewhere specified, e.g., the right to travel abroad. Kent v. Dulles, note 58 above. It has had a revival in the guise of a right of "privacy." See note 59 above.

64. Cf. United States v. Carolene Products Co., 304 U.S. 144, 152 n. 4 (1938); see generally Frankfurter, J., dissenting in Kovacs v. Cooper, 336 U.S. 77, 89 (1949). Also Kramer v. Union Free School District no. 15, 395 U.S. 621 (1969); Sherbert v. Verner, 374 U.S. 398 (1963); Roe v. Wade, 410 U.S. 113 (1973); and Shapiro v. Thompson, 394 U.S. 618 (1969). Cf. Henkin, "Privacy and Autonomy," pp. 1410, 1430. (1974).

65. See cases note 38 above; Nebraska Press Ass'n v. Stuart, 427 U.S. 539 (1976). But cf. Central South Carolina Chapter Society of Professional Journalists v. Martin, 556 F. 2d 706 (4th Cir. 1977), *cert. denied,* 98 Sup. Ct. 749 (1978); Leach v. Sawicki, Ohio Sup. Ct. 1977, *cert. denied,* 98 Sup. Ct. 729 (1978).

66. See Civil Rights Act of 1964, 78 *Stat.* 241, 42 U.S.C. sec. 2000 a (1970); Heart of Atlanta Motel v. United States, 379 U.S. 241 (1964). Cf. Congressional protection of the right to join a labor union, e.g., the National Labor Relations Act, 49 *Stat.* 449 (1935), as amended, 29 U.S.C. sec. 151 (1970); NLRB v. Jones & Laughlin Steel Corp., 301 U.S. 1 (1937).

67. See the Voting Rights Act of 1965, 79 *Stat.* 437, 42 U.S.C. sec. 1973 (1970); South Carolina v. Katzenbach, 383 U.S. 301 (1966); Katzenbach v. Morgan, 384 U.S. 641 (1966).

68. Jones v. Alfred H. Mayer Co., 392 U.S. 409 (1968); Runyon v. McCrary, 427 U.S. 160 (1976); Monroe v. Pape, 365 U.S. 167 (1961); also United States v. Guest, 383 U.S. 745 (1966); Griffin v. Breckenridge, 403 U.S. 88 (1971). Compare the case, eventually settled out of court, against federal officials who allowed several hundred syphilitic patients to go untreated so that they could be used as a control group in a medical research experiment. *New York Times,* December 15, 1976.

69. Freedom of Information Act, 80 *Stat.* 250, 5 U.S.C. sec. 552 (1976).

70. Universal Military Training and Service Act sec. 6(j), 69 *Stat.* 223 (1955), 50 U.S.C. sec. 456(j) (1970), as interpreted in U.S. v. Seeger, 380 U.S. 163 (1965).

71. E.g., National Environmental Policy Act of 1969, 83 *Stat.* 852, 42 U.S.C. sec. 4321 (1970).

72. E.g., Human Rights Law, N.Y. Executive Law sec. 290 et seq. (McKinney 1972); Environmental Conservation Law, N.Y. Envir. Conserv. Law (McKinney 1973).

73. Lochner v. New York, 198 U.S. 45 (1905); Adkins v. Children's Hospital, 261 U.S. 525 (1923); Allgeyer v. Louisiana, 165 U.S. 578 (1897); Carter v. Carter Coal Co., 298 U.S. 238 (1936); United States v. Butler, 297 U.S. 1 (1936); Pollock v. Farmers' Loan and Trust Co., 157 U.S. 429 (1895). These cases were later overruled (or essentially abandoned) in West Coast Hotel Co. v. Parrish, 300 U.S. 379 (1937); Nebbia v. New York, 291 U.S. 502 (1934); United States v. Darby, 312 U.S. 100 (1941); Steward Machine Co. v. Davis, 301 U.S. 548 (1937). See also note 28 above. The *Pollock* case was "repealed" by the Sixteenth Amendment.

74. Marx suggested that only in "a higher phase of communist society," "can the narrow bourgeois horizon of rights be left far behind" and will society inscribe these now famous words on its banner. Marx, *The Critique of the Gotha Programme* (1933) 31. Earlier Louis Blanc said, "Let each produce according to his aptitudes and his forces, let each consume according to his needs." *Organization du Travail* (1840). Compare p. 88, this chapter and note 123 below.

75. Compare Keyes v. School District no. 1, Denver, 413 U.S. 189 (1973); Moose Lodge no. 107 v. Irvis, 407 U.S. 163 (1972).

76. See Henkin, *Foreign Affairs and the Constitution* (1972) 257-259, 494-495.

77. See notes 38, 65 above.

78. Red Lion Broadcasting Co. v. F.C.C., 395 U.S. 367 (1969) ("fairness doctrine"); cf. Beauharnais v. Illinois, 343 U.S. 250 (1952) (upholding "group libel" laws).

79. Compare Regents v. Bakke, 98 Sup. Ct.—(1978); see "The DeFunis Symposium," 75 *Colum. L. Rev.* 483 (1975).

80. See, e.g., Lord Scarman, *English Law: The New Dimension* (1974), pt. 2; Lord Hailsham, *The Dilemma of Democracy* (1978).

81. Compare, for example, Colombia, p. 85 above.

82. For a recent article, see Phillips, "Self-Limitation by the United Kingdom Parliament," 2 *Hast. Const. L. Q.* 443 (1975). And see note 80.

83. See generally Cappeletti, *Judicial Review in the Contemporary World* (1971); idem, *Judicial Review in the Modern World: A Comparative Study* (1968); Clark, "Judicial Protection of the Constitution in Latin America," 2 *Hast. Const. L. Q.* 405 (1975). France and Germany provide for judicial review without awaiting a case or controversy and a private objector who has the requisite standing.

84. Cf., generally, Benda, "New Tendencies in the Development of Fundamental Rights in the Federal Republic of Germany." 11 *John Marshall J. Practice & Procedure* 1 (1977).

85. Compare Roe v. Wade, note 34 above, with the decision of the German court, *New York Times,* February 26, 1975; also the constitution of Ecuador (1972), Article 30; cf. Article 4(1), the American Convention on Human Rights, Chapter 3 below.

86. France practiced detention in Algeria, and Great Britain was found responsible for inhuman and degrading methods of interrogation in Northern Ireland. Cf. Report of a Committee to Consider, in the Context of Civil Liberties and Human Rights, Measures to Deal with Terrorism in Northern Ireland (Lord Gardiner, chairman), Cmnd. no. 5847 (1975); see O'Boyle, "Torture and Emergency Power under the European Convention on Human Rights: Ireland v. The United Kingdom," 71 *A. J. I. L.* 674 (1977).

87. U.S. v. Reiser, 394 F. Supp. 1060 (D.C. Mont. 1975), *reversed,* 532 F. 2d 673 (9th Cir. 1976), *cert. denied,* 429 U.S. 838 (1976).

88. See Clark, "Judicial Protection."

89. See, generally, G. de Ruggiero, *The History of European Liberalism* (Collingwood tr. 1927), especially pp. 370-394.

90. Sweden does not have judicial review; the "ombudsman" protects against bureaucratic illegality but will not limit parliamentary action or even top-level executive decision. See, generally, Gellhorn, *Ombudsmen and Others* (1966). Israel has an independent judiciary but no constitution for its courts to enforce. India has had judicial review but during its hiatus in freedom, the constitution was amended to curtail it sharply. See note 116 below. It has been noted that in those libertarian socialist and near-socialist states, there is a healthy "private sector" in the economy, and some would not call one or more of those states "socialist" at all. In Sweden libertarianism antedated socialism.

91. Article 2. See also Article 2 of the 1975 constitution. Cf. the Cuban constitution, Chapter 2, pp. 73-74 above.

92. See Marx, *Early Writings* (Livingston and Benton trans. 1975) 228-231; see also Chapter 1, note 42, and note 74 this chapter.

93. See Chapter 3, pp. 114, 126.

94. For a comparison of the 1975 Chinese constitution with the earlier constitution of the USSR, and for a discussion of Soviet criticism of China's constitution, see Hazard, "A Soviet Model for Marxian Socialist Constitutions," 60 *Corn. L. Rev.* 985 (1975).

95. Paine 93.

96. Paine 213.

97. See Hazard, Butler, and Maggs, *The Soviet Legal System* (3rd ed. 1977) 119-121.

98. Cf. Joint Anti-Fascist Refugee Comm. v. McGrath, 341 U.S. 123 (1951); New York Times Co. v. United States, 403 U.S. 713 (1971). See Henkin, *Foreign Affairs and the Constitution* (1972) 486-487, n. 7.

99. By law and regulation rather than by constitutional command, some access is provided to the electronic media, and antitrust laws help prevent press monopoly. Compare Red Lion Broadcasting Co. v. FCC, 395 U.S. 367 (1969) and Miami Herald Publishing Co. v. Tornillo, 418 U.S. 241 (1974); Associated Press v. United States 326 U.S. 1 (1945); see B. Schmidt, *Freedom of the Press v. Public Access* (1976), especially Chapter 4.

100. See Hazard, Butler, and Maggs, *The Soviet Legal System*, pp. 84, 96-104. Compare: "In our state, naturally, there is and can be no place for freedom of speech, press and so on for the foes of socialism. Every sort of attempt [to use these freedoms to the detriment of the state] must be classified as a counterrevolutionary crime." A. Vyshinsky, *The Law of the Soviet State* (Babb trans. 1948) 617.

Cf. Article 13 of the 1975 Chinese constitution: "Speaking out freely, airing views fully, holding great debates and writing big-character posters are new forms of carrying on socialist revolution created by the masses of the people. The state shall ensure to the masses the right to use these forms to create a political situation in which there are both centralism and democracy, both discipline and freedom, both unity of will and personal ease of mind and liveliness, and so help consolidate the leadership of the Communist Party of China over the state and consolidate the dictatorship of the proletariat."

101. Even more explicit and farther-reaching was the original constitution of the RSFSR (1918). Section 23 provided: "Being guided by the interests of the working class as a whole, the Russian Socialist Federated Soviet Republic deprives all individuals and groups of rights which could be utilized by them to the detriment of the socialist revolution." *Constitutions of the Communist Party-States* (J. Triska ed. 1968) 2, 5.

102. See 1954 Constitution, Articles 76, 78, 85, 90. Compare Jones, "A Possible Model for the Criminal Trial in the People's Republic of China," 24 *Am. J. Comp. L.* 229 (1976).

The 1978 constitution added a provision for secret ballot in the election of deputies to the National People's Congress (Article 21). The use of people's assessors in administering justice was restored (Article 41). Also reinstated was the freedom to engage in scientific research, literary and artistic creation and other cultural activities (Article 52). The right of men and women to marry of their own free will was added in 1978 (Article 53).

103. *History of Freedom and Other Essays* (Figgis and Laurence eds. 1916) 84.

104. According to Sakharov, "At least 10-15 million people perished in the torture chambers of the NKVD from torture and execution." *Progress, Coexistence and Intellectual Freedom* (1968) 52. According to Solzhenitsyn, "In addition to the toll of two world wars, we have lost, as a result of civil strife and tumult alone—as a result of internal political and economic 'class' extermination alone—66 (sixty-six) million people!!!" *Letter to the Soviet Leaders* (1974) 30. Medvedev has said that Solzhenitsyn exaggerates, the correct number being only 25-26 million. Quoted in Radio Liberty's Samizdat Archive no. AS 1874, p. 13, cited in *Survey,* vol. 21, no. 3 (Summer 1975): 134.

105. The Soviet Penal Code of 1966 makes it a crime to disseminate fabrications defaming the Soviet state (Article 190/1) or to organize and participate in groups that disturb order (Article 190/3), quoted in Hazard, Butler and Maggs, *The Soviet Legal System,* p. 97. An Amnesty International report stated that these articles were held to be violated by involvement in production, or even possession of *samizdat* (underground publications), sending letters of protest to the Soviet government or to international organizations, participating in demonstrations, sending manuscripts abroad. Those accused of these offenses may be kept in pretrial custody for more than a year, and Amnesty found no record of any defendant's being acquitted. See Amnesty International, *Prisoners of Conscience* (November 1971). Medvedev found "many serious shortcomings" in the administration of justice, including politicized, closed trials, vague crimes lending themselves to abuse ("anti-Soviet agitation and propaganda," "hooliganism," "parasitism"), and the use of psychiatric measures against dissenters; he saw the need to reduce the authority of the internal security forces. Medvedev, *On Socialist Democracy* (E. de Kadt trans. and ed. 1975), Chapter 8.

106. *Reflections on the Revolution in France* (1910) 93.

107. The texts of the constitutions cited are in the Blaustein and Flanz, *Constitutions*; and in Peaslee, *Constitutions of Nations*. See also D. H. Bayley, *Public Liberties in the New States* (1964); I. Duchacek, *Rights and Liberties in the World Today: Constitutional Promises and Reality* (1973); *Comparative Human Rights* (R. P. Claude ed. 1976).

108. See, e.g., Paul, "Some Observations on Constitutionalism, Judicial Review and Rule of Law in Africa," 35 *Ohio State L. J.* 851, 857 (1974). Cf. Seidman, "Judicial Review and Fundamental Freedoms in Anglophonic Independent Africa," ibid., p. 820; idem, "Constitutions in Anglophonic Sub-Saharan Africa: Form and Legitimacy," 1969 *Wis. L. Rev.* 83. Also International Commission of Jurists, *Human Rights in a One-Party State* (1978).

109. Chief Justice Marshall said the American Constitution was not to be reduced to "a splendid bauble." McCulloch v. Maryland, 17 U.S. (4 Wheat.) 316, 421 (1819).

110. Sri Lanka (1972, Article 18[2]).

111. Yugoslavia (1974, Article 153); Iraq (1970, Article 26); cf. similar limitations on freedom of speech in the constitutions of the USSR and Cuba above.

112. See, e.g., "Latin America—Expulsion, the Rights to Return, Passports," *The Review*, International Commission of Jurists, no. 14, June 1975, p. 3.

113. Sec. 6, Act 83 of 1967.

114. *New York Times*, July 6, 1975.

115. *New York Times*, November 30, 1975.

116. The Indian constitution was amended, inter alia, to give parliament plenary power to amend the constitution; to deny judicial review for individual rights; judicial review for violations of other provisions of the constitution was limited to the Supreme Court, and invalidation required a two-thirds vote. See *New York Times*, November 3, 1976. This amendment has not been repealed to date, but efforts in that direction have been indicated. See *New York Times*, June 14, 1977.

117. *New York Times*, October 19, 1975.

118. For an imaginative effort to conceptualize the study of human rights conditions and construct a schema for appraising them, see Dominguez, "Assessing Human Rights Conditions," in J. I. Dominguez et al., *Enhancing Global Human Rights* 1978. Borrowing a matrix of eight values (enlightenment, skill, well-being, respect, affection, rectitude, wealth, and power), Dominguez would

judge a political society as to each under four criteria—growth, equality, liberty, and security.

119. See Chapter 3.

120. In 1976 a Freedom House report on political freedom in the world concluded that less than 20 percent of the people in the world were free, that 35.3 percent were partly free, and that 44.9 percent are not free. This represented a sharp decline in freedom in only one year—due mainly to the political crisis in India. See R. D. Gastil, "Comparative Survey of Freedom, VI," *Freedom at Issue,* no. 34 (January-February 1976), p. 11. Freedom was rated higher in the 1977 report largely owing to the reversed situation in India. See also the annual Associated Press reports on freedom of the press around the world, e.g., *New York Times,* January 25, 1978.

121. Beginning in 1977 the U.S. Department of State has been reporting to Congress on the condition of human rights in countries that receive or are candidates for U.S. aid. See Chapter 3, note 50. There are also periodic official and semiofficial reports on the implementation of the human rights provisions of the Helsinki accord, Chapter 3, note 13.

Generally reliable reports on notable developments, particularly on dramatic violations, appear occasionally in the press and more fully in the reports of various nongovernmental organizations such as Amnesty International (which issues monthly newsletters, an annual report, and occasional special reports), the International Commission of Jurists, and the International League for Human Rights. Other, more specialized organizations issue reports on the human rights of people with whom they are particularly concerned; for example, Jewish organizations report regularly on the rights of Jews in the Soviet Union.

122. See Chapter 3. Compare Strouse and Claude, "Empirical Comparative Rights Research: Some Preliminary Tests of Development Hypotheses," in *Comparative Human Rights* (R. P. Claude ed. 1976), Chapter 2.

123. Compare Vlastos, "Justice and Equality," in Melden, *Human Rights* (1970) 76-95.

Chapter 3

1. See H. Lauterpacht, *International Law and Human Rights* (1950, 1973) Part 1, Section 2. There are also links between the antecedents of international law and of natural law in ancient Rome. See Chapter 1, note 58.

In this chapter, I draw on several articles I have written: "The Internationalization of Human Rights" in *Human Rights, A Symposium*, Columbia University Committee on General Education (1977); "Human Rights: Readjustment and Reappraisal," in *Human Rights, Contemporary Issues and Jewish Perspectives* (D. Sidorsky ed. 1978); "Human Rights and 'Domestic Jurisdiction' " in *Human Rights, International Law and the Helsinki Accord*, (T. Buergenthal ed. 1977); "The United States and the Crisis in Human Rights," 14 *Va. J. Int'l L.* 653 (1974).

Bibliography and other sources on themes struck in this chapter are available in Sohn and Buergenthal, *International Protection of Human Rights* (1973). For a brief history of the early growth of international protection of human rights, see Schwelb, *Human Rights and the International Community* (1964).

2. Powerful countries sought to protect their nationals against denials of justice in some countries by "capitulation agreements" whereby the "sending state" was given exclusive jurisdiction over offenses committed by their nationals.

3. Minorities provisions had been imposed also in the nineteenth century by the Congress of Berlin, when it recognized the independence of Romania (and others); they were also included in peace treaties following World War II, e.g., with Austria. There are also bilateral reciprocal agreements to respect minorities, e.g., between India and Pakistan. References to rights of minorities are also contained in various UN resolutions and conventions. See Sohn and Buergenthal, *International Protection of Human Rights*, Chapter 4.

4. Articles 22 and 23. Also, Article 2 of the mandate for South-West Africa, for example, provided: "The Mandatory shall promote to the utmost the material and moral well-being and the social progress of the inhabitants." These provisions have been generally held to be violated by the imposition of apartheid. See note 35 below, and, generally, Sohn and Buergenthal, *International Protection of Human Rights*, Chapter 5.

5. See International Labor Organization, *Chart of Ratifications: International Labor Conventions*, January 1, 1978.

6. It soon appeared, however, that self-determination did not eliminate minorities and the problem of minorities. It apparently does not necessarily include the right to secede, e.g., by Biafra. Its exercise and implementation in various parts of the world have not in fact eliminated minorities, and many new states were formed that created or perpetuated minorities. Whether in old states or new,

moreover, individual rights have not always flourished for all, and minorities often suffered more than others.

Human rights later developed to include particular rights of special concern to minorities, e.g., cultural and linguistic freedom, and rights for the group. Compare Van Dyke, "Human Rights and the Rights of Groups," 18 *Am. J. Pol. Sci.* 725 (1974).

7. See L. Henkin, *How Nations Behave* (1968), Chapter 2.

8. For the development of these provisions, see Sohn "A Short History of United Nations Documents on Human Rights," in *The United Nations and Human Rights,* Eighteenth Report of the Commission to Study the Organization of the Peace (1968) 43.

9. U.N. Doc. A/810, December 10, 1948. Text in Appendix. Other declarations and conventions followed. See pp. 97-101 above, and Schwelb, *Human Rights.*

10. Cf. Chapter 2, pp. 78 et seq. above.

11. On the nonbinding character of the Declaration, see Lauterpacht, *International Law,* Chapter 17. But cf. ibid., pp. 405-406; see Sohn, "A Short History," p. 71. On the authority and impact of the Declaration, see Sohn and Buergenthal, *International Protection of Human Rights,* pp. 518-522.

12. E.g., G. A. Res. 1904 (XVIII), November 20, 1963, Article 11.

13. Final Act, Conference on Security and Cooperation in Europe, Helsinki 1975, "Declaration on Principles Guiding Relations between Participating States," 1(a) VII.

14. Compare M. Cranston, *What Are Human Rights?* (1973).

15. For recent developments in economic self-determination, see the Charter of Economic Rights and Duties of States, G. A. Res. 3281 (XXIX), December 12, 1974, and the "Declaration and the Establishment of a New International Economic Order," GAOR Sixth Special Session, Supp. no. 1, Res. 3201, 3202 (S-VI), May 1, 1974.

16. Although property is not expressly protected, the Covenant on Economic Social and Cultural Rights permits developing countries to deny economic rights under the Convention to nonnationals. Article 2(3).

17. On the development of the covenants, see, generally, Sohn, "A Short History"; Schwelb, *Human Rights;* Schwelb, "Some Aspects of the International Covenants on Human Rights of December 1966," in *International Protection of Human Rights,* Proceedings of the Seventh Nobel Symposium, September 1967, Eide and Schou eds. (1968) 103; A. H. Robertson, *Human Rights in the World* (1972), Chapter 2.

18. See Chapter 2.

19. For a brief description of these and others, see Schwelb, *Human Rights,* p. 40. More recently, in 1973, the UN General Assembly also adopted the International Convention on the Suppression and Punishment of the Crime of *Apartheid,* G. A. Res. 3068 (XXVIII), November 30, 1973, in force July, 18, 1976.

20. The Refugee Convention may also be effectively joined by way of a protocol. See note 36 below. As of early 1978, sixty-eight states have adhered to the Convention and sixty-three to the protocol, many to both. For a full record of adherences to the various agreements, see Multilateral Treaties in Respect of Which The Secretary-General Performs Depository Functions, as at December 31, 1977 U.N. Doc. ST/LEG/SER. D. 11, and supplements.

21. Cf. p. 97 this chapter above.

22. Cf. the report of the International Law Commission on the work of its twenty-eighth session, May 3-July 23, 1976, GAOR, 31st Sess. Supp. no. 10 (A/31/10) pp. 226 et seq.

23. See Henkin, *How Nations Behave,* Chapters 3-6.

24. Ibid., p. 42.

25. See Henkin, "Human Rights and 'Domestic Jurisdiction.' "

26. In the Covenant, it is binding only on states that make a declaration to that effect, Article 41; submission to this procedure is automatic in the Racial Discrimination Convention, Article 11. Compare the institutions and procedures of the European and American conventions, this chapter pp. 103-105 above. "State-to-state" complaints before a designated body are optional also under the American Convention, Article 45.

27. See the Optional Protocol to the Covenant on Civil and Political Rights, Article 14 of the Convention on the Elimination of All Forms of Racial Discrimination; Article 25 of the European Convention, pp. 103-104 this chapter. It is not optional in the American Convention, Article 44.

28. See, e.g., Covenant on Civil and Political Rights, Article 40.

29. See Res. 1503 (XLVIII), Economic and Social Council, May 27, 1970.

30. See Chapter 2, notes 120-121 above; also, for example, Scoble and Wiseberg, "Human Rights and Amnesty International," 413 *Annals* 11 (1974).

31. For a comparison of the European Convention with the UN Covenant, see Robertson, *Human Rights in the World,* Chapter 4. See generally ibid., Chapter 3; also A. H. Robertson, *Human Rights in Europe (1976);* C. Morrisson, *The Developing European Law of Human Rights* (1967); F. G. Jacobs, *The European Convention on Human Rights* (1975).

Some human rights advances in Europe have resulted also from other common ventures—for example, from the bill of rights NATO developed for members of foreign forces accused of crime. See North Atlantic Treaty Status of Forces Agreement, June 19, 1951, [1952] 4 U.S.T. 1792, T.I.A.S. no. 2846, Article VII.

32. Article 21. See, generally, Robertson, *Human Rights in the World,* Chapter 5.

33. See A. Schreiber, *The Inter-American Commission on Human Rights* (1970); L. LeBlanc, *The OAS and the Promotion and Protection of Human Rights* (1977); Buergenthal, "The Revised OAS Charter and the Protection of Human Rights," 69 *A.J.I.L* 828 (1975); and the annual reports of the Inter-American Commission on Human Rights.

34. In 1968-1969 the Arab League established a Permanent Commission on Human Rights. It has given priority to the questions of the rights of Arabs living in territory occupied by Israel, but apparently plans a general program of promoting human rights in the region. An African commission is also burgeoning. See Robertson, *Human Rights in the World,* Chapter 6.

35. Ethiopia and Liberia brought an action against the Republic of South Africa in the International Court of Justice for violating its mandate in South-West Africa, note 4 above. But South Africa has generally been an object of political attack and of "unfriendly relations." And the provision invoked, in a League mandate, was claimed to give rights to other states against the mandatory power, but not reciprocal obligations and remedies between states generally. After many years, the court dismissed the action. [1966] *I.C.J. Rep.* 6. See generally S. Slonim, *South West Africa and the United Nations: An International Mandate in Dispute* (1973).

36. A Soviet author summarizes as follows:

> The Soviet Union and the other socialist countries seek to ensure that this cooperation should be directed towards the genuinely democratic development of rights and freedoms for all, without distinction as to race, nationality, sex and religion, on the basis of freely concluded equal agreements.
>
> They at the same time adhere to the position that international agreements must not contain clauses infringing the sovereign rights of States independently to define the rights and obligations of their citizens in accordance with their economic and social characteristics. Nor should agreements contain clauses establishing any supra-State agencies dealing with human rights and having legislative, administrative or judicial functions.

K. Y. Chizhov in *International Law,* published by the Academy of Sciences of the USSR Institute of State and Law, Moscow, pp. 137-138, quoted in Przetacznik, "The Socialist Concept of Protection of Human Rights," 38 *Social Research* 337, 340-341 (1971). See, generally, *Socialist Concept of Human Rights* (J. Halasz ed. 1966), published by the Institute for Legal and Administrative Sciences of the Hungarian Academy of Sciences.

A provision for compulsory jurisdiction of the ICJ in the Convention relating to the Status of Refugees is not subject to reservations, but that was believed to discourage adherences; a principal reason for a strange device making it possible to adhere to that Convention indirectly through a protocol (note 20 above) was the desire to make it possible to enter a reservation to that clause and accept the Convention without it. Cf. Articles 38, 42(1) of the Convention, July 28, 1951, 189 U.N.T.S. 137, with Articles IV and VII of the Protocol, January 31, 1967, 606 U.N.T.S. 267. On the reluctance to accept jurisdiction of the ICJ generally, see Henkin, *How Nations Behave,* pp. 174-175.

37. See UN Covenant on Civil and Political Rights, Article 41. As of January 1, 1978, only Denmark, Finland, Norway, Sweden, Great Britain, and the Federal Republic of Germany had made the necessary declarations. But parties to the Convention on the Elimination of All Forms of Racial Discrimination submit to such complaints automatically (Article 11). See note 26 above.

38. See note 27 above. The Covenant and the Protocol went into effect on March 23, 1976. The following states were party to the Protocol when it came into effect: Barbados, Colombia, Costa Rica, Denmark, Ecuador, Finland, Jamaica, Madagascar, Mauritius, Norway, Sweden, and Uruguay. Canada, Panama, Surinam, and Zaire have since adhered.

39. See p. 102 above.

40. UNGA Res. 32/130, December 16, 1977.

41. See, e.g., the report that Chile supported an Arab anti-Zionist resolution in the UN in exchange for Arab support for Chile in defending itself against charges of torture and other serious human rights violations. *New York Times,* October 19, 1975.

42. See Liskofsky, "International Protection of Human Rights," in *World Politics and the Jewish Condition* (Henkin ed. 1972), Chapter 8, pp. 297-300. On the politicization of human rights generally, see also Bilder, "Rethinking International Human Rights," 1969 *Wis. Law Rev.* 171.

43. See this chapter p. 99n. above.

44. See, e.g., "The Control of Program Content in International Communication," 13 *Colum. J. Transnational L.* 1 (1974).

45. See *New York Times*, December 10, 1977, and December 8, 1977.

46. On the United States and human rights generally, see the symposium in 14 *Va. J. Int'l L.* 591 et seq. (1974); also in the special supplement 7 *Ga. J. Int'l and Comp. L.* 219 et seq. (1977).

47. Since World War II, the United States has adhered only to the Geneva "Red Cross" Conventions, the updated Convention on Slavery, the Protocol relating to the Status of Refugees, and the Convention on the Political Rights of Women. In part, our poor record is due to apathy and to resistance by domestic political forces reflected in the Senate. For example, the Genocide Convention has lain on the shelf of the Senate since 1949, and another effort to obtain Senate consent was killed by filibuster in February 1974. See 120 *Cong. Rec.* 2334-2339 (1974). Later efforts languished from resistance and apathy in the Senate and unwillingness by the executive to exert pressure and expend political capital to attempt to overcome them. In 1977 President Carter signed the Covenant on Civil and Political Rights (but not the Protocol), and the Covenant on Economic and Social Rights. These and other conventions were sent to the Senate on February 23, 1978, but with troubling reservations.

48. But compare France, which delayed its adherence to the European Convention for many years, ratifying finally in 1974, with important reservations. See Coussirat-Coustère, "La réserve française à l'article 15 de la Convention Européenne des Droits de l'Homme," *Journal du Droit International*, 1975, no. 2, p. 269.

49. During 1973-1975, Congress, on the initiative of a subcommittee and of Representative Donald Fraser of Minnesota, in particular, promoted greater awareness and responsiveness by the Department of State. See U.S., Congress, House, Committee on Foreign Affairs, Subcommittee on International Organizations and Movements, *Human Rights in the World Community: A Call for U.S. Leadership*, 93rd Cong., 1st sess., 1974.

50. The International Security Assistance and Arms Control Act of 1976 includes extensive expressions of U.S. policy to promote and encourage increased respect for human rights and fundamental freedoms, and to deny security assistance to foreign governments that engage in "a consistent pattern of gross violations of internationally recognized human rights." The president is directed to formulate and conduct security assistance programs so as to further these policies and to avoid identification of the United States with governments

that deny human rights. The secretary of state must report to Congress on human rights observance in countries proposed as recipients for security assistance. Upon congressional request, the secretary must transmit to Congress all available information about human rights in recipient countries and about the steps the United States has taken to promote respect for human rights there and to dissociate itself from any violations; he must also indicate any extraordinary circumstances that warrant continued security assistance to a violating country. Congress also established in the State Department a coordinator for human rights and humanitarian affairs. Section 301 (a), Pub. L. no. 94-329, 1976, 22 U.S.C.A. secs. 2304, 2384, 2151n. (1976). See also the earlier provisions, International Development and Food Assistance Act of 1975, sec. 310, Pub. L. no. 94-161, 89 *Stat.* 849; section 502 B of the Foreign Assistance Act of 1974, P.L. no. 93-559, 88 *Stat.* 1815. Compare also Section 301 (b) of the 1976 Act, 22 U.S.C. sec. 2314(g), designed to discourage discrimination by recipient foreign governments against American nationals on account of race, religion, national origin, or sex.

Congress has also sought to use foreign assistance to promote "maximum participation in the task of economic development by the people of less developed countries through the encouragement of strong economic, political and social institutions needed for a progressive democratic society"; and to promote private enterprise, political stability, and economic, social, and political reform. Pub. L. no. 90-137, 81 *Stat.* 448 (1967); Pub. L. no. 92-226, 88 *Stat.* 26 (1972), 22 U.S.C.A. secs. 2167(a), 2168(b), (c), (f), 2218, 2346. See Weissbrodt, "Human Rights Legislation and United States Foreign Policy," 7 *Ga. J. Int'l and Comp. L.* 231 (1977).

51. Compare pp. 111, 115 above, this chapter. See generally "Alternative Approaches and Ways and Means within the United Nations System for Improving the Effective Enjoyment of Human Rights and Fundamental Freedoms," Report of the Secretary General, UN Doc. A.10235, October 7, 1975, and Report of the Third Committee on the same subject, A/10404, December 3, 1975.

52. The clause has been used to encompass all matters that are not regulated by international law. Compare, e.g., the United States' reservation to its declaration under the optional clause accepting the jurisdiction of the International Court of Justice, [1946-47] I.C.J. Y.B. 217-18, 228.

53. "Near-constitutional" but not quite. Compare Dandridge v. Williams, 397 U.S. 471 (1970); San Antonio Ind. School District v. Rodriguez, 411 U.S. 1 (1973).

54. See International Commission of Jurists, *Human Rights in a One-Party State* (1978).

55. G.A. Res. 32/130, December 16, 1977, note 40 above.

Chapter 4

1. See Chapter 3, pp. 102, 109-110 above.

2. H. Lauterpacht, *International Law and Human Rights* (1950, 1973), p. 131.

3. In other respects, however, Burke still speaks to our time. See, for example, A. Bickel, *The Morality of Consent* (1975), especially Chapter 1.

4. Paine, I guess, would be ahead of most in seeing human rights large, to include all that goes into a life with dignity. Compare Chapter 1, p. 24 above.

5. Quoted in Collins introduction, T. Paine, *Rights of Man* (H. Collins ed. 1969) 47.

DATE		
DEC 0 7 1982		
NOV 1 2 1985		
DEC 8 '86		
OCT 3 0 1990		
APR 2 4 1991		
APR 1 0 2001		
10-14-03		

© THE BAKER & TAYLOR CO.